The Parties Versus the People

The Parties

Versus

Yale UNIVERSITY PRESS   NEW HAVEN & LONDON

the People

How to Turn Republicans and Democrats into Americans

Mickey Edwards

Published with assistance from the Louis Stern Memorial Fund.

Yale University Press books may be purchased in quantity for educational,
business, or promotional use. For information, please e-mail
sales.press@yale.edu (U.S. office) or sales@yaleup.co.uk (U.K. office).

Set in Janson Roman type by Integrated Publishing Solutions.
Printed in the United States of America.

Library of Congress Cataloging-in-Publication Data
Edwards, Mickey, 1937–
The parties versus the people : how to turn Republicans and Democrats into
Americans / Mickey Edwards.
p.   cm.
Includes bibliographical references and index.
ISBN 978-0-300-18456-3 (hardcover : alk. paper)   1. Political parties—
United States.   2. Democracy—United States.   3. Polarization (Social
sciences)—United States.   4. Two-party systems—United States.   5. Di-
vided government—United States.   I. Title.
JK2265.E38 2012
320.973—dc23
2012013008

A catalogue record for this book is available from the British Library.

This paper meets the requirements of ANSI/NISO Z39.48–1992
(Permanence of Paper).

10 9 8 7 6 5 4 3 2

To Bill Budinger, whose vision and generosity are helping to create an American politics based on common purpose and mutual respect. And to the more than 150 public leaders who are members of the Aspen Institute's Rodel Fellowship.

Contents

Contents

Preface

Year after year, through nearly two decades and ten national elections, American voters have grown angrier and more frustrated with a government that they theoretically control. After all, they are citizens, not subjects, and they live in a democracy. The presidents and the members of Congress with whom they are so disappointed are the very men and women they themselves have chosen. Yet when national elections are held, these voters go to the polls and repeatedly cast their votes for "something different," for "change," for what golfers call a "mulligan," a do-over. A government that once met, and solved, enormous challenges, overcoming the inevitable disagreements between competing philosophies, no longer does so. Differences have hardened into polarization, and simple party identification has been overtaken by a rigid partisanship. Presidents, governors, and state legislators engage actively in partisan combat, but the Congress, where the problem is worst and the effects most damaging, has become utterly dysfunctional, unable to come together on almost any issue of national importance. There are many causes for this evolution, but at its root the problem is systemic. As I will show in these pages, we have been unable to overcome the effects of these changes because we conduct our elections, and our leaders attempt to govern, in a political system that makes common effort almost impossible to achieve.

Voters are resilient: like Charlie Brown, determined to kick his football knowing full well that Lucy will probably once again pull it away, they persist in trying to fix a government that seems to now be intractably, and dangerously, unable to come to agreement on almost anything. Some years voters hand power to Democrats and some years they elect Republicans; they try candidates who have long and impressive business or government résumés, or they may choose candidates who substitute youth, dynamism, or "new ideas" for the experience they lack. But whichever choice the voters make, our government no longer seems to work as it once did. One group of elected leaders may adopt policies that another group might not have enacted, federal spending may go up or down, taxes may rise or fall, and our national budget priorities may change, but beneath it all American government today functions not as a collective enterprise of citizens working together to solve our common problems, but as a never-ending battle between two warring tribes.

The damage is greatest in the Congress, which, with 435 members in the House of Representatives and 100 in the Senate, requires a degree of good faith cooperation and compromise that no longer exists. But it is also true in the White House where, no matter who is president, teams of legislative and political advisers map political strategies to attack opponents rather than seek common ground across party lines. And it is true as well among the governors and legislators in the states, with minority party members sometimes fleeing their states altogether to prevent legislative action because neither party is able or willing to hammer out necessary compromise. This is not a problem that can be laid at the feet of one political party or one set of public officials; it is the result of a fundamental flaw in the way we conduct our elections and in the way those who are elected must subsequently govern. That flaw—the attempt to govern a diverse nation with a system based on a partisan war for control—has grown steadily worse in recent decades. In the world of the twenty-first century, it has worsened to a degree that seriously threatens our system of self-government.

I first presented the argument I will make here in an annual "big ideas" issue of the *Atlantic;* it was the magazine's editors who gave that article the title "How to Turn Republicans and Democrats into Americans."[1] Too often our elected leaders seem to think of themselves not as trustees for America's future but as members of a political club whose principal obligation is to defeat other Americans who do not share an allegiance to the same club. As a result, after every election we discover yet again that our political "leaders" don't lead; they quarrel, slinging verbal and legislative missiles at each other and threatening to punish any deserters who cross over to the other side. What we thought was a democratic government made up of leaders committed to the national good has turned into a new form of contact sport, an attempt to score more points than the other team by any means possible. Meanwhile, our bridges grow old and collapse, our banks and investment houses pursue policies that cripple our economy, and we become ever more dependent on Chinese money and Middle Eastern oil.

This persistent partisan dysfunction has been analyzed, dissected, hashed, and rehashed for more than a decade, and countless books, articles, blogs, and broadcasts have assessed blame and offered prescriptions. All of them are wrong. They blame the people we elect ("Where are all the leaders?") or the people who elect them (too apathetic, too profligate, too penurious), the money that is spent on political campaigns (which is, in fact, a significant part of the problem but not the root of it), the media, the appalling lack of civics education in our public and private primary and secondary schools and in our universities, and the failure to teach critical thinking. Each of those things is a contributing factor, but each one ignores the cancer at the heart of our democracy.

Most political commentators today (except those who themselves fuel the partisan wars) complain endlessly about the polarization that has become evident in the American political system, and there is considerable evidence that Americans have tended in recent years to sort themselves into communities of like-minded souls. Conservatives dominate some regions of the country, liberals others. In many cases, we and our friends tend to read the same opinion articles, vote similarly, and seldom engage in serious conversation with people whose political views differ from our own. But it is not this political segregation that is driving the dysfunction in Washington. For one thing, it is wrong to conclude that those politically segregated groups are necessarily extreme. Even a separateness that inhibits serious consideration of divergent viewpoints does not mean that the voters within these camps are mindlessly hostile to alternatives or compromise. As University of Chicago professor Geoffrey Stone has pointed out, 40 to 45 percent of Americans "are more or less moderate in their views."[2] The nation's leading political pollster, Andy Kohut, president of the Pew Research Center, has made a similar point, noting that while both major parties contain significant numbers of philosophical hard-liners, the vast majority of voters are more moderate (and thus, one might suppose, amenable to compromises that might break through the partisan gridlock).

As Stone told the American Academy of Arts and Sciences in 2011, "Understanding polarization requires a closer look at how Congress is constituted. In 1970, 47 percent of the members of the U.S. Senate were regarded as moderate. Today, that figure is 5 percent, and it is even lower in the House of Representatives. The decline of moderate views in Congress suggests a kind of dysfunction:

a dramatic gap between the views and attitudes of the American people and the commonalities and differences that exist among our citizens, on the one hand, and what we wind up with in our elected representatives, on the other. Something is going wrong in our politics."

Precisely. The dysfunction that has almost paralyzed our federal government has its roots not in the people, not in any fundamental flaw in our constitutional processes, but in the political party framework through which our elected officials gain their offices and within which they govern.

It is not my goal, therefore, to take the easy path of simply blaming "polarization," the most common description of the problems that plague our political life. To the extent that to be polarized is to inhabit the extreme reaches of a viewpoint, it is clear that the greater the degree of polarization—the more voters there are on the far right and the far left—the harder it will be to come together in the national interest. Zealots do not compromise. But most experts agree with Kohut and Stone that while a number of Americans reside on the political fringe, a great many more do not. It should be relatively simple to say to those who do, "Howl at the moon if you wish . . . but in the meantime the rest of us will govern the country." But if such a large voting population is amenable to a search for common ground, why is that common ground so hard to reach? It's because the problem is not the extent of polarization but the extent of partisanship, and the two are not the same thing. As I will argue in this book, it is the party system—Democrats against Republicans, not liberals against conservatives—that is at the heart of our political mess.

Consider the important issues with which the nation has grappled just since the beginning of the Obama presidency. When the Obama administration proposed to address deteriorating conditions in the economy by an infusion of federal spending, virtually no

Democrats found the proposal unacceptable and virtually no Republicans found it acceptable. When Democratic Senator Christopher Dodd of Connecticut and Democratic Congressman Barney Frank of Massachusetts drafted a plan to increase oversight of financial institutions, Republicans were united on one side, Democrats on the other. Plans to reframe the government's role in health care pitted a solid phalanx of Republicans against an equally cohesive army of Democrats. Budget deliberations fell apart because Democrats were almost uniformly lined up in supporting higher tax rates for citizens who earn more than $250,000 annually per couple and Republicans were equally unified on the other side. The same thing happened with consideration of the president's nominations for seats on the Supreme Court. In a sane world, in which the men and women we elect to Congress apply their own research and intelligence to the important decisions that confront them, we would expect some number of Republicans to vote with Democrats and some Democrats to line up with Republicans. But on the big issues, the ones that matter most, solid blocs face other solid blocs, unmovable, unflinching in their loyalty to the party "team." And that is because of the framework within which our politics unfolds. As we will see, party leaders control important committee assignments, provide or withhold money for reelection campaigns, and advance or block team members' legislative priorities; in our political system, one often pays a significant price for exercising independent judgment.

This book is not about the symptoms of our dysfunction but about the system in which our government functions. A brief analogy: baseball teams that play in extraspacious stadiums, with great distances between home plate and the outfield walls, consciously develop strategies to accommodate that reality. They forgo trying to build teams that are dependent on home-run hitters and instead develop lineups made up of players who are adept at hitting singles and stealing bases; these teams also don't feel the need to find pitchers who are good at inducing opposing batters to hit ground balls because most fly balls are likely to remain in the ballpark. On the other hand, teams that play in smaller stadiums, where home runs are easier to hit, fill their lineups with power hitters; but because visiting teams likewise will find it easier to hit home runs, the small-stadium team will try to sign pitchers who are adept at inducing opposing batters to hit ground balls. In other words, the system within which one plays affects the outcome. That's true in politics, too. If the game of government rewards intransigence and punishes compromise, we shouldn't be surprised if we get a lot of intransigence and not much compromise. Incentives work: if the greatest incentives are to behave badly, we will get bad behavior. If our government continues to fail us—and it will—then we need to change the incentives, change the architecture of the field on which we play.

In the world of political science, many academics have argued that strong political parties, dominated by strong party leaders, are essential to democratic governance. As long ago as the 1950s, a number of prominent voices within the American Political Science Association were urging greater party homogeneity based on the belief that efficiency and accountability—the power to enact one's preferences and the corresponding ability of voters to know who to blame if things didn't work out—are the principal requirements of a governing system. This is, in fact, a transposition to America of European-style parliamentary systems, in which voters, in essence, elect ideologies, not representatives, and it is a convenient formula, subject to the easy measurements that the academic world requires. But it leaves little room for legislators to serve as the voice of those who have elected them (thus ignoring the Founders' clear intention that members of Congress be familiar with the interests of the voters they represent and that the voters likewise be familiar with the candidates who seek their votes). The parliamentary model leaves little room for the fair interplay of competing interests. In parliamentary systems, voters choose to hand great power to a single political faction, with the voters' only recourse being the periodic ability to remove that faction from power; the American model of representative democracy, which is very different, is designed to give voice to a multiplicity of factions and to allow for competing views to be weighed, often resulting in compromises designed to balance interests. It is precisely for that reason that the rigid partisanship which today inhibits compromise is so destructive.

In one sense the party solidarity that has developed in recent years differs from the model that many political scientists advocated: they equated party strength with strong party leaders who would dictate to their followers what was expected of them and use various carrot-and-stick tools to ensure compliance. Today's party strength is bottom-up: although during the Newt Gingrich Speakership—the one that most closely followed the blueprint the academics desired—the Speaker was a bully and called the shots, in today's Congress, considerably more power rests with the party caucus. Party leaders may or may not prevail in determining who will run under the party label; instead, party activists will make that decision. Many academics argue that parties today are weak, but that is because they equate "party" with "party leader." These are different things. Party leaders may be strong (Gingrich) or constrained (current Speaker John Boehner), but the ability of party primaries, party-controlled redistricting, and caucus-enforced party solidarity to shape the political landscape is indisputable.

What follows in this book is a different way of looking at things. It's about etiology, not observable effect. I will not shock anybody with my assertion that our political system is broken, at times seemingly beyond repair. That the system is annoyingly unresponsive to our frustrations, and that our leaders often seem unwilling to try very hard to address the nation's problems (and appear incapable of doing so even when they do try), seem self-evident. Political columnist Mary Curtis has written that the people want their representatives "to grow up . . . they wish leaders would spend as much time figuring out how to solve the country's problems as they do plotting to be king of the playground."[3] Except in times of national emergency—and not always then—common effort seems beyond us. The essentials of a pluralistic democracy—reasoned debate and a probing examination of policy options—have been replaced by unreasoned and uncivil squabbles.

In this book I intend to look at why the people we elect spend so much time "plotting to be king of the playground." It's not because they're stupid or uncaring—it's because of the field on which they play and the rules that govern the game. We have engendered a political system in which the necessary and inevitable "interest-based factions" the Founders anticipated, understood, and worried about have been supplanted by permanent factions whose primary focus is on gaining and retaining political power.

In the *Federalist No. 10*, James Madison argued for ratification of the Constitution largely on the grounds that it would provide a bulwark against the fractious spirit that had "tainted" the previous workings of government. He described the evil against which he hoped to inoculate the new government as "a number of citizens, whether amounting to a majority or a minority of the whole, who are united and actuated by some common impulse of passion, or of interest" who would be adverse to "the permanent and aggregate interests of the community." It is a perfect description of the political parties that have come to dominate the politics of the twenty-first century.

It is my aim in this book to describe how to end the parties' control over the process by which we govern ourselves. My goal is not necessarily to create a more moderate or more centrist Congress, though that might be one of the end results of the reforms I propose, and this might actually be a more accurate reflection of the electorate. At the same time, changing our system to guarantee that neither women nor African-Americans would be denied the right to participate in the election process was not the work of centrists; it was a radical reform. So were the efforts to mandate that workers be paid a living wage. I am not proposing a system that would drive serious reform out of the discussion.

Nor is this book about increasing voter turnout, though that, too, might result from the reforms I propose. Professor Alan Abramowitz of Emory University convincingly argues, with the support of considerable research, that among "engaged" voters—voters who pay attention and participate—those who prefer Republicans are farther to the right than they used to be, and those who favor Democrats are farther to the left than in the past.[4] Abramowitz also finds that among those who are most engaged, more than half identify strongly with a specific political party. Although he does not make this point, clearly it is those "engaged" voters who participate in our current system of closed party primaries; and if those primaries determine our available choices in the November elections, we will thus likely have more conservative, or more liberal, elected officials than if we can increase the number of choices available to the voters—and thereby make participation more attractive to voters who prefer neither extreme. That, not a mere increase in the number of voters, should be the goal.

Finally, I am not objecting to the fact that the Congress does not move more swiftly than it does nor that it does not pass more legislation. Peter Baker of the *New York Times*, referring to what he called a "standstill nation," wrote that "it's useful to remember that the founders devised the system to be difficult, dividing power between states and the federal government, then further dividing the federal government into three branches, then further dividing the legislative branch into two houses. The idea, James Madison wrote, was to keep factions from gaining too much power . . . and to be sure, gridlock is in the eyes of the beholder . . . one person's obstructionism is another's principled opposition."[5] When a government is contemplating taking more from its citizens in taxes, or eliminating its support for the suffering, or sending its citizens to war, or permitting police to track a citizen's every movement without a search warrant or an assertion of "probable cause," moving too speedily or doing too much can pose a great danger; taking time for thoughtful deliberation is an indispensable virtue. Vigorous conflict over competing values, principles, and policies is a strength, not a weakness, of democracy. This book is not about avoiding dissent but about avoiding conflict that is based on party rather than principle.

My aim is to open up the process to give American voters more choice and more voice, and to eliminate the partisan forces that limit options and dilute representation. I wish to restore *democracy* to our democracy. That is not as hard a task as it may seem: a few simple changes are all that's required. In these pages I will describe what those changes are and how to make them happen.

Acknowledgments

Ever since a constituent berated me for blaming "the other party" for the failures in Washington—and was greeted with loud applause for doing so—I have found myself thinking often about the role party rivalry plays in the increasing inability of our elected officials to work together in search of common ground. I don't remember that constituent's name, but he's at the top of the list of those to whom I'm indebted.

I have discussed this concern over the years with a number of men and women whose opinions I respect greatly, including several of my colleagues during the years when I taught government at Harvard and Princeton. After I left full-time teaching I continued to teach occasional night classes at Georgetown University, George Washington University, and the University of Maryland, and had many interesting discussions with my students about their frustrations with the current political environment. I have also had long discussions with former and current members of Congress and with many of the outstanding young elected officials who make up the

Rodel leadership program I now direct for the Aspen Institute. It would take another book just to mention them all.

Congressional scholars Lou Fisher and Don Wolfensberger, Virginia Sloan and Steve Hanlon of the Constitution Project, and Nancy Jacobson of No Labels all gave me good advice and much to think about. Jeanine Plant-Chirlin of the Brennan Center at New York University was part of this project from the very beginning, and her help was indispensable as it moved from an idea to a magazine article to, finally, this book. I learned a lot from Frank Barry, whose excellent book about Progressive Party politics I cite in these pages. I pestered my friend Sean Theriault, of the LBJ school at the University of Texas, to read drafts of articles and newspaper columns (Sean has written his own excellent book about party politics). Scott Olson helped with research and was fast and dependable. Kathleen Godfrey became a critical part of the project, and her help was invaluable. Gia Regan is, technically, the assistant director of the Rodel Fellowships, but she's far more than that; I cannot imagine how I could have written this book without her help.

I am frequently invited to speak at universities and to business, professional, and academic groups; in the process I have bounced my concerns, and my ideas, off of thousands of bright men and women, with each such occasion sharpening my thinking and strengthening my resolve to write this book. I thank all of them, particularly the participants with whom I interacted in programs at the Montpelier Institute, the Academy of Arts and Sciences, The Carnegie Council for Ethics in International Affairs, New York University's Brademas Center for the Study of Congress, and Harvard's Center for American Political Studies. Conversations with former Supreme Court Justices Sandra Day O'Connor and David Souter helped me sharpen my thinking. So, too, did my conversations with Geoff Stone of the University of Chicago and Akhil Amar and Heather Gerken of Yale.

Liftoff came when James Bennet, editor of the *Atlantic*, asked me to put my ideas into an article for the annual "Big Ideas" issue of the magazine. The article generated an enthusiastic response and James, more than anyone else, gets the credit for helping elevate the argument I make here. The *Atlantic*'s James Gibney took on the task of working with me to reduce my original draft to magazine length and made the article, and consequently the book, much better than what I had sent to him.

Allison Stanger, whose excellent book *One Nation Under Contract* I had admired and praised, not only helped me think through my conclusions but led me to her editor, William Frucht of Yale University Press. If there's such a thing as an indispensable editor, it's Bill Frucht. Lucky is the author who gets to work with him.

Lucky, too, is the man who gets to be married to Elizabeth Sherman. She's my partner, my best friend, my Lizzie.

PART I

Partisan Poison

ONE

American Tribalism

We have strayed far from the political system the Founders envisioned. Sean Wilentz, in *The Rise of American Democracy*, notes that James Madison worried that "the arts of electioneering would poison the very fountains of liberty."[1] Madison understood that in the end, democracy is not about policy but about process—it's about how we select our leaders, how we deliberate, how we decide—and it is the process itself that has broken down. The partisan poison that has seeped into American politics—and American governance—is not only eroding belief in the democratic process, it is proving to be a danger to the very idea of participatory self-government. Democracy, after all, is not a spectator sport—it requires active citizen participation—but partisanship, which is not a conflict over principle but a combat between private organizations, each seeking political advantage, is creating a system which stirs not confidence but rage. Peter Shane, a professor at Ohio State University, wrote a book he called *Madison's Nightmare*.[2] His particular focus was on the growing power of the executive branch and the diminished power of the "peoples' branch," but the title was apt: if the dead can have nightmares, James Madison and the rest of America's founders are having an uneasy afterlife as they observe what we have done to the political system they left us. They had many disagreements among themselves, but they all agreed on the inherent danger in political parties. While it's true that parties came into being early in the nation's history, they were nothing like the ones we have today; their members were united on some major issues, but not on everything all the time. Ironically, there is diversity within Republican and Democratic ranks in today's Congress, too, but the system in which they are forced to operate enforces conformity, not independent thinking. As Alan Abramowitz of Emory University points out, our system of government was not designed to function with the kind of partisan division that exists today; instead, the Founders saw political parties as "dangerous fomenters of conflict."[3] Today we have become accustomed to seeing straight party-line votes on everything from tax issues and spending issues to judicial and executive branch appointments. It is not the existence of parties but the excessive loyalty members of Congress feel to the parties they belong to, and the great power we have given parties over our elections and our governance, that have led us to the crisis we are in today, unable to come together even on the most urgent questions, and even with the nation's well-being at stake.

How we got to this point is not hard to understand. As the American political party system took root throughout the 1800s, it became harder and harder for a democratically minded people to accept the idea that small groups of insiders—party bosses—should be able to gather in the back rooms of private clubs to determine who should carry the party's banner in the next election, whether for mayor, governor, or the U.S. Senate or House of Representatives. In a democracy, the reformers argued, the people themselves should be empowered to make those decisions. The result was a campaign by members of the Progressive movement, culminating in the early 1900s, to have party nominees chosen in primary elections in which all registered party members could participate. By 1916 all but a handful of states had instituted the "direct primary" system, in which each party's candidate was selected by public vote rather than by party leaders in backroom deals. But the primaries, and the nominating conventions, were open to party members only. This reform was supposed to give citizens a bigger role in the election process. Instead, the influence of party bosses has now been supplanted by that of a subset of party activists who show little interest in finding common ground with those who hold different views.

In the Progressive Party platform of 1912, the goal was spelled out clearly. "This country belongs to the people who inhabit it. . . . Political parties exist to secure responsible government and to execute the will of the people. From these great tasks both of the old parties have turned aside. Instead of instruments to promote the general welfare, they have become the tools of corrupt interests which use them impartially to serve their selfish purposes. Behind the ostensible government sits enthroned an invisible government owing no allegiance and acknowledging no responsibility to the people." Declaring itself "unhampered by tradition . . . undismayed by the magnitude of the task," the party, in its very first platform plank, called for "direct primaries for the nomination of State and National officers." On that goal, against great odds, the Progressives won; the result was a major improvement over the system of boss rule, and it was certainly far more democratic. But it presupposed that the results of those primaries, or of party conventions in the states that chose that hybrid system (less democratic but also less elitist), would provide an accurate reflection of the preferences of the larger electorate. As Francis Barry points out in his 2009 book, *The Scandal of Reform: Grand Failures of New York's Political Crusaders and the Death of Nonpartisanship*, that has not always been the case; in fact, those reforms have had a profound, and sometimes negative, effect on the democratic process.[4] As the system has evolved, partisan primaries have become powerful magnets for the most committed, and most ideological, voters. Conservatives and liberals alike use the closed primary system to move their parties farther toward the positions of the far right and far left and ever more distant from what political scientists call the "median voter."

At the same time, as the government expanded into more areas of our lives and inevitably grew more controversial, it also became much more complex, with the issues and the arguments increasingly difficult for any but experts to understand. The growing force of money in political campaigns has also caused many citizens to conclude that their own limited ability to participate in the decisions would make little difference, making it hardly worth the effort required to vote. Except in unusual circumstances, such as the 2008 presidential campaign of a young African-American candidate and widespread disaffection with an outgoing Republican presidency, the great mass of eligible voters has chosen not to participate in party primaries, which have thus become reflections not of public choice, as the Progressives had intended, but of ever narrower and ever more ideological agendas. "Party" has become a synonym for rigid, uncompromising, narrow "faction." And we are paying a very steep price for it.

To picture just how dysfunctional our political system has become, imagine how you and your neighbors would set about the task of solving some important problem in your community. Suppose, for instance, that a new neighborhood organization has been established for the specific purpose of improving the schools in your town, and that you and your neighbors have come together out of a common concern for the children in your community, whose lives will be largely shaped by the education they receive. Assume that you and your neighbors are already working to ensure that only highly qualified teachers are hired and are actively encouraging the students' parents to enforce good study habits at home. But there is still more that the community can do. The children need ample and well-lighted classroom space, a large supply of up-to-date textbooks, modern computer equipment, a well-equipped science laboratory, an adequate physical education facility, and so on. In other words, you will be faced with a serious challenge, and how well you meet that challenge will have a noticeable impact on your community, including, perhaps, your own children.

Now imagine how you would go about meeting that challenge. When your new organization meets to address these important goals, you will consider many things. What equipment is needed? What space is needed? Does that require a new building? If so, where should it be located? Who should design it and build it? How can the necessary resources be accumulated? Can some person or some organization be found to donate the computers, books, and gym equipment? As you attempt to meet these important community goals, people in the group will be invited to make suggestions, to ask questions, to discuss options. But there is one thing you will probably not do: you will probably not divide the organization into separate partisan camps, with Republicans in one group and Democrats in another. There will probably be no attempt to choose task force leaders or remove members from the organization on the basis of membership in one or the other political club.

And yet when our actual elected officials consider whether to spend more on medical research or public education, to repair our aging bridges and highways, or to send our children to fight in foreign wars, or when they consider whether to take more or less from us in the form of federal taxes, that is precisely what they do: they begin by dividing into rival camps on the very day they are sworn into office. It is their differences—their partisan affiliations—and not their commonality as Americans that shapes the process. Compromise, an absolutely indispensable ingredient in a highly diverse nation of more than 320 million people, is seen as "sell-out"; rigid uniformity is praised (many members of the United States Senate brag about voting with their party 90 or 95 percent of the time). The scarlet letter "A" on Hester Prynne's dress was no greater a mark of opprobrium in the eyes of her fictional contemporaries than the wearing of an imagined red letter "R" or "D" attached to a member of a rival political party.

The political parties' "main fear," *New York Times* columnist David Brooks has written, "is that they will lose their identity and cohesion if their members compromise with the larger world. They erect clear and rigid boundaries separating themselves from their enemies. In a hostile world, they erect rules and pledges and become hypervigilant about deviationism. They are more interested in protecting their special interests than converting outsiders. They slowly encase themselves in an epistemic cocoon."[5]

Just as in the tragic turf wars between the Jets and the Sharks in *West Side Story*, members of the other political club are seen as enemies to be slain, if only figuratively, at the ballot box and in battles over public policy decisions. When that happens—and it is now the norm—the tragedy is not theirs but ours.

The bitter partisanship that envelops our modern politics is a natural result of a political system that cedes so much power to self-serving private clubs, but while its most obvious effect is the difficulty in finding the common ground necessary to create sound public policy, it has had other damaging ramifications as well. Ours is a system in which it is possible for one party to hold 40 percent of the seats in the United States Senate and 49 percent of the seats in the House of Representatives (because of partisan redistricting, those legislative "minorities" may actually represent a majority of

American voters) and yet have no real power to affect policy out-comes. Members of the majority party in Congress not only deter-mine the legislative agenda, they also control all committees and subcommittees; the chair, always a member of the majority party, no matter how narrow the majority, has the sole power to determine what bills will be considered and whose opinions will be solicited during committee hearings. In the House of Representatives, mem-bers of the minority party usually have only that degree of input that the majority allows. As a result, winning control of the Congress, and even of state legislatures (where congressional districts are shaped) becomes essential. In such a system, members of the other party become not merely rivals but enemies. Civility, a basic re-quirement for democratic dialogue, disappears in a tidal wave of acrimony and insult.

While partisanship is certainly not the only cause of the incivility that has poisoned public discourse (the declining standards of the broadcast media, which fuel conflict in pursuit of ratings, and the tendency of Americans to shut themselves off from views they dis-agree with—well-documented in Bill Bishop's important work, *The Big Sort*—also share a large part of the blame), the focus invariably centers on the political arena, where the choices about government policy are made.[6] The inability to come together on bipartisan ap-proaches to solving national problems also stirs frustration, anger, discontent, and a lack of confidence in American government and its constitutional system, as those important problems persist and grow worse year by year. While members of the various Tea Party organizations and the activists of Occupy Wall Street might be fo-cused on different parts of the problem—an overwhelming national indebtedness and failure to enforce immigration laws, perhaps, for the Tea Party; tax inequities and disproportionate influence in the political system for the Occupiers—they have at their root a com-mon genesis: important problems that go unaddressed because our political system has devolved into a ceaseless campaign in which our elected officials are always playing to the audience that their campaign strategists believe will be most likely to shape the next election's outcome. In such a scenario, members of Congress—and presidents—play to their parties' base, which is increasingly made up of the most rigidly ideological and uncompromising segments of the electorate.

Ironically, as our leaders wage their continuing war over party advantage, the American people themselves are headed in the opposite direction. In April 2010 *USA Today* reported on a nationwide poll that found that "a majority disapprove of both political parties."[7] More Americans now consider themselves Independents than either Republicans or Democrats, with more than four in ten voters registered as Independent, Unaffiliated, or Unenrolled. When a little-known Republican state legislator, Scott Brown, won the Massachusetts U.S. Senate seat that had been held by Edward Kennedy for more than four decades, observers outside the state were stunned; not only had the Senate seat been Ted Kennedy's, but the state had not elected a Republican to the Senate since Edward Brooke won his race for a second term in 1973, thirty-seven years earlier. But Massachusetts is no longer a predominantly Democratic state; today the number of Massachusetts residents registered as Unenrolled (that is, Independents) is greater than the number registered in either the Republican or Democratic party.

This rejection of our political parties—and their constant partisan warfare—has been growing for years. As early as November 2006, a *Wall Street Journal*/NBC News poll showed that fully 42 percent of voters nationwide considered themselves Independents.[8] Between 1987 and 2004, the number of Independent voters in Florida quadrupled.[9] Another survey of twenty-seven states plus the District of Columbia found that the number of Independents in those states had doubled. Independents outnumber both Republicans and Democrats in Alaska, Connecticut, Iowa, Maine, Massachusetts, New Jersey, and New Hampshire.[10] The lead story in *USA Today* on April 20, 2010, was headlined "Frustrated Voters Cut Tie with Democrats, Republicans" and began this way: "The nation's fastest-growing political party is 'none of the above' . . . more Americans are registering 'unaffiliated' rather than signing up with one of the two major parties."[11] The story went on to report that in at least half of the twenty-eight states in which voters register by party, the number of Independent voters had increased faster than that of either Democrats or Republicans in the previous two years. In Arizona, the number of Independent voters had increased by nearly one-third between 2008 and 2010. A 2010 Gallup poll found that both major parties are now viewed unfavorably by most Americans.[12] "People no longer want to be associated with a party," New Hampshire's elections director, Gary Bartlett, told a reporter for *USA Today*.[13] Some observers have pointed out that many of those who now call themselves Independents are not without political leanings toward one party or another, but even among those who may be more likely to vote for a Republican or a Democrat the party tie has been severely weakened: they are no longer part of the party "base"; they can no longer be depended on for their vote. Their votes are up for grabs, and that's the way it should be.

As a member of Congress I relied heavily on frequent town or neighborhood meetings to stay in touch with my constituents, who were usually not at all hesitant to let me know what they were thinking. At one such meeting, more than twenty years ago, a man in Oklahoma City demanded to know why I had not succeeded in achieving some policy goal that both he and I supported. I followed the script: as a Republican, I blamed congressional Democrats, who were then in the majority and who therefore determined what legislation would be able to receive consideration in committee and on the House floor. I got no sympathy, either from the man who asked the question or from the others in the meeting room: "I'm sick and tired of hearing Republican this, Democrat that," he said, and the room erupted in applause. Needless to say, I never gave that answer again. Except for those activists who gain disproportionate power through our closed primary system of elections, the American people have been becoming less partisan even as their elected officials continue to draw hard lines in the sand, resisting compromise and fighting for party advantage.

We cannot go on this way. We need to restore a sense of common purpose both in the federal government—in Congress and in the presidency—and in our state legislatures. Democracy requires an openness to diverse opinion and a fostering of vigorous debate. But it also requires that each participant in that debate use his or her knowledge, experience, and judgment to make decisions for the public—not the partisan—good.

Clearly, our democracy does not work this way today. Our elections don't seem to change anything because we elect our leaders, and they then govern, in a system that makes cooperation almost impossible and incivility nearly inevitable. It is a system in which the campaign season never ends and the struggle for party advantage trumps all other considerations. Listening to my car radio soon after Democrat Nancy Pelosi became the Speaker of the House of Representatives, the leader of the lawmaking branch of government, I heard her tell a reporter that her goal was to . . . elect more Democrats. After the Republican victories in the midterm elections of 2010, the Senate's Republican leader, Mitch McConnell, said his goal was to . . . prevent the Democratic president's reelection. "The single most important thing we want to achieve is for President Obama to be a one-term president," McConnell told the *National Journal*. During the prolonged congressional debate over Obama's health care reform plan, Republican Senator Jim DeMint of South Carolina, noting the bill's unpopularity with much of the public, gloated that the plan would prove to be Obama's "Waterloo." When McConnell and DeMint made those statements, the country was at war and the economy was sinking into recession. With many Americans homeless or unemployed, with high federal deficits, these government leaders' first thoughts were of party advantage.

This is not an accident. Ours is a system that has become focused not on collective problem-solving but on a struggle for power between two private organizations. As I will discuss in this book, party activists control access to the ballot through closed party primaries and conventions; partisan leaders design congressional districts; once they are elected to Congress, our representatives are divided into warring camps from which partisans decide what bills to take up, what witnesses to hear, what amendments to allow. We have become so accustomed to thinking of government this way that C-SPAN, the television and radio network that broadcasts both the House and Senate sessions and a variety of public policy conversations, routinely instructs its listeners to call in on either "the Republican line," "the Democrats' line," or "the Independents' line" as though all important national issues must be viewed through a partisan lens.

Many Americans assume that's just how democracy works, that this is how it has always been, that it's the system the Founders created. But what we have today is a very far cry from what those men intended. George Washington, John Adams, Thomas Jefferson, and James Madison—our most important Founders and our first four presidents—all warned of the great dangers posed by political parties. Defenders of the party system point out that parties—including Madison's own party—arose almost immediately after the nation was founded. But those were not parties in the modern sense; they were factions united on a few major issues, not marching in lockstep on every issue, large or small. As I will discuss in more detail, what we have today is not a legacy of 1789 but an outdated relic of the late 1800s and early 1900s, an outgrowth of what was once a well-intended and important reform that has, over the years, turned into a dark force that threatens the very survival of our deliberative democracy.

What I propose in these pages is a new system in which citizens are allowed full freedom to unite in common cause with those who agree with them, and in which parties are allowed full freedom to express their preferences (I do not oppose the existence of parties, nor their right to argue on behalf of their preferred candidates)—but with one very important difference: political parties would no longer control either the election process or the governing process. Political parties would still exist; they would be welcome to participate but not to dictate. Some, primarily political science theorists, have responded to the proposals I lay out here by arguing that there is no actual evidence that they will increase voter turnout, or lead to the election of more "moderates," or strengthen third parties. But those are not my goals: voters will turn out if they believe that the results of our elections will affect their lives and that their participation can affect which policies will eventually be enacted; they will vote for moderates—or conservatives, or liberals—if those are the candidates who best represent their views. Third, fourth, or fifth parties will be supported if they present better candidates or better proposals than the Republicans or Democrats they run against. My goal is not to determine "who" voters vote for, but to give them a greater range of choices: in other words, to expand democracy.

I have not always held the positions I express in these pages. For a good many years, I held, and I tried to defend, a very different view. As a young man, I was a political activist and I engaged in my activism largely through the political party system. In my home state of Oklahoma, I filled a variety of party roles—organizing, attending, and chairing precinct meetings; serving on and chairing party platform committees; attending and chairing party conventions. As a member of the Young Republicans, I chaired a local club and then a statewide club, and ultimately became a vice president of the national organization, each step as part of a partisan "team." I attended national party conventions, served as a cochair of a party platform subcommittee, worked the national convention floor on the behalf of the candidates I preferred. I supported my party's positions in print and on the air. Later, as a member of Congress, I worked with the party's campaign committee; served as one of the party's regional "whips," lining up votes for the party's positions; and moved up in the ranks of party leadership, eventually becoming the chair of my party's policy committee in the United States House of Representatives. I had many good friends among the Democrats in the House and Senate (a wonderful experience that today's strongly divided legislature makes much more difficult), but I was nonetheless very much a party person. As the overall director of congressional policy task forces for Ronald Reagan's 1980 presidential campaign, I was fully engaged in the partisan political conflict.

But I came to the conflict indirectly. Like most who enter the political arena, I had given a lot of thought to questions such as the proper relationship between citizen and government, the purposes and missions of government, the proper size and scope of a national government, the balance between individual liberty and a citizen's collective responsibility to the larger community, the difference between government and community, etc. In other words, when I entered into government myself, I did so with a clear sense of what I thought was right, and I was a party member only because I believed that the party I had chosen to join offered me the best means of achieving the ends I thought the times required. I was "in" the party but not "of" it; my loyalty was to my own principles, not to the club I was a part of, and even as a member of the party's leadership I toed the party line only if it fit well with my own conclusions as to what was the right thing to do. I simply could not imagine how one could, in good conscience, support a party position one did not agree with. I could not conceive of how I, as a sworn member of Congress, could support a president, even of my own party, if I thought he was doing the wrong thing. As members of Congress, doesn't the oath of office, and an obligation to the citizens who elected us, mean anything? As the years went by, my ties to the party in which I was then one of the highest-ranking elected leaders began to fade slowly but surely, though I seldom gave public voice to those thoughts. When the party adopted positions that I considered to be not only "bad government" but also, on their face, unconstitutional, and did so out of a desire to achieve political advantage, I demurred but watched in amazement as most of my colleagues went along with what seemed like a good political strategy, even if a blatant violation of their oath of office.

I later taught for sixteen years, first at Harvard and then at Princeton. Some of my friends who have been disturbed by my drifting from party loyalty have accused me of drinking too deeply from the waters of the Charles River in liberal Massachusetts, spending too much time among pointy-headed Harvard theorists who spend their days in cloistered lives divorced from real-world realities. But here is what that experience gave me: time to back off, to reflect, to consider what I had observed, to think more deeply about what did, and did not, work—and about why American government had become so dysfunctional. The more I thought about it, the greater the clarity. The political system does, in fact, work; it works very well; it does precisely what it is designed to do. What we have created is a process in which the incentives reward those who cater not to the polity as a whole but to small and zealous subgroups who demand a rigid adherence to very narrow objectives, who punish deviation (in other words, thinking for oneself), and who, as a reward for conformity, limit the opposition that one faces in a general election by restricting ballot access through the unseemly and indefensible power our states have surrendered to self-serving political clubs. The government we have is dysfunctional in regard to the proper functions of governance, but it is scarily functional in following the trajectory that our political system rewards.

Three states, most recently California in 2010, have voted to strip the parties of much of their power over the political system, an important and hopeful development. All across America, new organizations have emerged to promote bipartisanship or nonpartisanship. I have worked with several of them, most notably with No Labels (of which I am a cofounder), an organization of more than 400,000 fed-up citizens who do not seek the elimination of party labels but who insist on public leaders whose focus is on problem-solving without regard to those labels. Many of the proposals I make in this book, about party primaries, about redistricting, even about changes within the Congress itself, have now been adopted as No Labels positions. I've mentioned earlier that much of what I offer here first appeared in the *Atlantic;* I was surprised by the strong—and overwhelmingly positive—reaction to that article, which was widely distributed, reprinted, and even posted in such unlikely places as a United Nations/World Bank web page for members of the world's parliaments. I hope here to show a path out of the partisan tribalism that has overwhelmed our ability to collectively solve our nation's problems, but it is clear that I am not alone in hoping to do so. What follows are suggestions designed to turn our political system on its head so that people, not parties, control our government. So buckle your seat belt, because half-measures, simply doing things as they've been done in the past, are not going to fix a political system that is so broken that every two years we try desperately to unfix what we thought we had fixed two years earlier. Neither you nor I have the time to bemoan the state of things: we need to fix it. And we need to do it now.

More than thirty years ago, the French philosopher and journalist Jean-François Revel wrote a book titled *How Democracies Perish.*[14] The topic was different (Revel was worried that the West was insufficiently prepared to counter what was then a very real challenge from the Soviet Union), but the title stuck with me—democracies can perish; they can disappear altogether or they can be twisted into forms increasingly disconnected from democracy's defining characteristics. In today's America, citizens typically are allowed to elect their public leaders from among the narrow menu of choices permitted by our political parties, and from districts drawn to serve party interests; and when these leaders take office—as our putative "representatives"—it is too often party, not constituent or conscience, that guides their performance. Yale law professor Akhil Amar notes that the United States was the first nation in history in which the people themselves were allowed to vote on how they would be governed.[15] What an irony it would be if in the democracy the people created, their own voices, and their own influence, were to be shunted aside, as private clubs elevated their own pursuit of power to the principal theme of modern political theater.

TWO

The Disappearing Dream

America's founders were well aware of the dangers inherent in a system of permanent rival factions. In the *Federalist No. 10*, arguing for adoption of a new constitution, James Madison cited complaints "everywhere heard" that "the public good is disregarded in the conflicts of rival parties, and that measures are too often decided, not according to the rules of justice and the rights of the minor party, but by the superior force of an interested and overbearing majority." His description of the problem seems eerily familiar today, noting that "a zeal for different opinions [and] an attachment to different leaders ambitiously contending for pre-eminence and power" had "divided mankind into parties, inflamed them with mutual animosity, and rendered them much more disposed to vex and oppress each other than to co-operate for their common good."

Madison wasn't alone in his cautions against political parties. In his farewell address in 1796, as he prepared to step down from the presidency, George Washington, too, warned of the hyperpartisans we now observe so clearly in our own time. "They serve to organize faction, to give it an artificial and extraordinary force; to put, in the place of the delegated will of the nation, the will of a party, often a small but artful and enterprising minority of the community."

The men who wrote the Constitution clearly intended that the votes of lawmakers be shaped by the constituencies they served, a goal made manifest by the requirement that senators and representatives be actual inhabitants of the states from which they are elected. Two hundred and fourteen years later, the *Washington Post* published a review of Senate voting records.[1] Over the previous two years, Congress had taken up important votes on America's wars in Iraq and Afghanistan, had approved billions of dollars of federal spending, and had wrestled with many controversial and difficult issues, about which we would hope our representatives would gather as much information as possible and carefully evaluate the prescriptions being proposed in order to cast a responsible vote.

During that two-year period, senators had cast more than 650 votes. The article in the *Post* noted that forty-four of the one hundred members of the Senate had voted with their party more than 90 percent of the time, and that twenty-four of them—a fourth of the Senate—had gone along with party policy more than 95 percent of the time. Dick Durbin of Illinois and Patty Murray of Washington had strayed on fewer than three votes out of a hundred—a 97.5 percent party purity rating. Ben Cardin of Maryland was loyal to his club 97.4 percent of the time. Others were similarly loyal: Chuck Schumer of New York (96.9 percent), Daniel Akaka of Hawaii (96.8), Frank Lautenberg of New Jersey (96.6), Sherrod Brown of Ohio (96.4 percent), and so on: Kohl, Bingaman, Levin, Menendez, Wyden, Reed, Whitehouse, Boxer, Dodd, Kerry, Cantwell, Leahy, Stabenow, Harkin—all true blue to the party label more than 95 percent of the time. Among the most strongly committed to following the party line were three who went on to other jobs: at the time of that accounting, Barack Obama, Joe Biden, and Hillary Clinton were still in the Senate, and they, too, were among the club faithful: Clinton, 97.3 percent of the time; Biden, 96.7 percent; and Obama, 96 percent.

While all those most loyal to the party line that particular year happened to be Democrats, clearly hanging together in opposition to George W. Bush's presidency and with an eye toward recapturing the White House, Republicans, loyal to their own party and to the Republican president, were less rigid to the party line only by the smallest of margins. Senator Johnny Isakson of Georgia departed from his team's party line on only seven votes out of a hundred. Mitch McConnell, Saxby Chambliss, John Cornyn, Craig Thomas, and Roger Wicker all stuck to the Republican line more than 90 percent of the time. (There were few exceptions: only seven—Olympia Snowe, Arlen Specter, Gordon Smith, Norm Coleman, Chuck Hagel, Richard Lugar, and George Voinovich—voted the party line on fewer than 80 percent of the votes; Specter was eventually forced to switch parties with the realization that he would be unable to defeat a more consistently conservative candidate in a Republican primary). Granted, people become Republicans or Democrats because they tend to agree more often than not with the policies of one or the other party, so it's natural that the majority of the time they would find themselves on the same side of an issue as others in their party. Yet it is inconceivable that, no matter their differences in experience, constituencies, and personal interests, they would find themselves on the same side of almost every issue time after time. It is clearly time for their constituents to demand to know whether these men and women believe it is their job to serve their party or the country. Considering the great amount of money and effort that had gone into the elections that produced these senators, perhaps it would have been wise instead to skip the elections and simply allow Senate Majority Leader Harry Reid and Minority Leader Mitch Mc-

Connell to cast those states' votes by proxy. At least the country would have saved the considerable cost of the salaries and the staffing of the offices of senators who, like Sir Joseph in *H.M.S. Pinafore*, "always voted at my party's call, and never thought of thinking for myself at all."

In recent years we have become accustomed to a political war that operates almost on autopilot. Partisans began the battle over retiring Supreme Court Justice David Souter's replacement even before the president had determined whose name he would submit to the Senate: members of one party knew they would support the nominee, no matter who he or she happened to be; members of the other party would oppose the nominee. Who it was didn't really matter. When Sonia Sotomayor was nominated to replace Souter, Republicans and Democrats predictably split along party lines, either to support a nominee against whom legitimate questions could be raised or to defeat her despite a successful and largely uncontroversial record as a federal judge who had once been almost unanimously approved by the very same Senate for a seat on the Federal District Court (as the stakes rose, partisanship reared its head; when Sotomayor was nominated for a seat on the Federal Court of Appeals, a step up from the District Court, she was opposed by all but seven of the Senate's Republicans).

After Justice John Paul Stevens announced his retirement plans in early 2010, and attention turned to the selection of a replacement, *Washington Post* columnist George Will noted "how recently and radically the confirmation process has changed."[2] Will pointed out that even in the Court's most controversial days, when President Franklin D. Roosevelt was battling to keep the Court from derailing his New Deal proposals, his nomination of Felix Frankfurter "sailed through Senate hearings and the confirmation vote in twelve days. It was a voice vote, with no audible dissent." Two months later, another FDR nominee, William O. Douglas, was confirmed in fifteen days. "No witness testified against him," Will observed.

Justice Stevens had been confirmed unanimously in 1975. In 1981, with Ronald Reagan in the White House and Democrats working feverishly to block his conservative initiatives, his Supreme Court nominee, Sandra Day O'Connor, was also confirmed unanimously. Antonin Scalia, another Reagan nominee, was confirmed unanimously in 1986.

In 1987, however, the Senate rejected another Reagan choice, Robert Bork. Perhaps there were ample reasons for the Senate's decision. Bork's understanding of the Constitution's First Amendment protections was disturbingly weak and, despite my own position within the Republican congressional leadership and my close ties to the Reagan White House, I, too, felt compelled to urge Bork's rejection. What was most noticeable, however, was not the Senate's failure to vote for confirmation, but how the senators divided on the issue. Despite Bork's long career on the federal bench, every Democrat except two voted against the nomination; despite his poor grasp of the Bill of Rights, every Republican but six voted to seat him on the Supreme Court of the United States. Partisan division had entered the decision-making process. Four years later, when President George H. W. Bush nominated Clarence Thomas, party line voting was back. One could argue that Thomas was a poor choice (little judicial experience, no impressive record of legal writing, allegations of improper conduct), yet Republicans backed him faithfully, 41–2. Although Thomas would have been only the second African-American Supreme Court Justice in the nation's history, Democrats voted against him by a ratio of better than four to one. Justices Anthony Kennedy (nominated after Bork's rejection), Ruth Bader Ginsburg, and Stephen Breyer were confirmed easily, but the partisan genie was not to remain bottled up for long, and it soon reappeared with a vengeance. John Roberts had compiled a distinguished record on the federal bench: every Republican in the Senate voted for his confirmation. Half the Senate Democrats, however, opposed him. When Samuel Alito was nominated, only one Republican voted against him and only four Democrats voted for him. There are differences between Republicans and Democrats when it comes to the prevailing party view about the role of the judiciary and how one defines legitimate "interpretation" as opposed to unwarranted judicial activism, and that difference affects the president's decision regarding whom to nominate and how senators view those nominations. But is it possible that in a Senate of a hundred members of varying experiences, constituencies, professions, ages, genders, shoe sizes, hair colors, ethnicities, and religions, there would be no more complexity than this: over and over again, Republicans on one side, Democrats on the other, no matter what? (To illustrate how dramatically party division has been exacerbated in the current age, consider that when the Senate refused to confirm two of Richard Nixon's Supreme Court nominees, the partisan division was far less stark. The confirmation of Clement Haynsworth, Jr., was defeated 45–55, with 19 Democrats and 26 Republicans voting for the confirmation, and 38 Democrats and 17 Republicans voting against. G. Harrold Carswell's nomination failed on a 45–51 vote, with 17 Democrats and 28 Republicans in support, and 38 Democrats and 13 Republicans opposed).

This shift is found well beyond the walls of the Supreme Court. President Dwight Eisenhower, a Republican, was a strong advocate of a new federal interstate highway system. In 1956, the Congress, with both houses controlled by Democrats, approved it overwhelmingly. Today it is almost impossible to conceive of a United States not bound together by its interstate highways, but at the time Eisenhower proposed the new system, there were ample concerns about the impact on the many communities that were connected by the existing two-lane highways that often ran right through the heart of town and brought travelers to the doors of local restaurants and retailers as well as to the much-needed gasoline filling stations. Not only would the new system change all that—bypassing towns altogether— but paying for it would require higher taxes. Yet in a Congress that was controlled by a party other than the president's, Republicans and Democrats were united in support. The House of Representatives voted in favor of the new highway system 388–19, and then, after the final details emerged from a compromise conference with the Senate, approved it again on a simple voice vote. The Senate approved its version of the bill on a voice vote and then, after the House and Senate bills had been combined, approved it again, 89–1.

In 1964, President Lyndon Johnson advocated a far-reaching civil rights act that would outlaw employment discrimination, discrimination in registering voters, and discrimination in public facilities. While few today would consider such protections controversial, that was not the case half a century ago. Many employers believed it was their right to use whatever standards they wished in choosing whom to hire; state officials believed it was within their authority, and outside the federal government's jurisdiction, to establish election procedures; merchants thought it within their purview to decide whom to accept as customers. Today one imagines that such a controversial subject might divide parties along predictable lines, with Democrats and Republicans trying to appeal to whomever they saw as their political "base." But that important vote was not held in 2012, when party warfare is continuous and party advantage determines policy preferences. It was held in 1964, and in both the House and Senate clear majorities of both Democrats and Republicans supported the legislation (Republicans by a larger percentage since the Democrats' majorities then included a sizable number of Southerners who resisted the changes). The point, here, however, is not merely that the legislation was approved but that even on such a significant and nation-altering issue, the vote did not divide along party lines.

In 1965, the Congress passed social security amendments that created a new Medicare entitlement program, the first major government involvement in what had historically been a purely private interaction between patients and their health care providers. It was a monumental policy shift, far more dramatic than the health care legislation that struggled through Congress in 2010 with Republicans and Democrats in sharp conflict. The vote in 1965? Though the Democrats were more united on the issue, and there was a Democratic president in the White House, a majority of both Republicans and Democrats voted yes in the House of Representatives. In the Senate, where Democrats were again more strongly in support of the proposition, Republicans divided almost equally.

Few pieces of legislation have had more effect on federal construction activities than the National Environmental Policy Act passed by Congress in 1969, establishing a new presidential council on environmental quality and instituting a requirement for environmental assessments and environmental impact statements for any construction activity proposed by a federal agency (lakes, highways, federal buildings, military bases, etc.). The legislation was passed by the House of Representatives 372–15; it passed the Senate unanimously. As far-reaching as the bill was—it laid the groundwork for today's much more expansive system of environmental protections—legislators did not divide into rival teams.

By contrast, consider congressional passage thirty years later, in January 2009, of the Lilly Ledbetter Fair Pay Act, which made it easier for employees to file lawsuits based on claims of pay discrimination. Again, whichever position one takes on the central question—whether or not a discriminated-against employee should be barred from suing because of a passed filing deadline—one might logically expect that if the men and women we elect to public office are thinking of their constituents' interests and evaluating proposals independently, there would be noticeable divisions within Democratic ranks and similar divisions among Republicans. Not in this hyperpartisan age: in the House of Representatives, which passed the Act 247–171, only three Republicans voted "yes" and only two Democrats voted "no." In the Senate, which approved the legislation 61–36, every Democrat voted "aye," and all but five Republicans voted "nay."

When the House of Representatives, in the middle of a recession, voted in 2009 to provide a financial stimulus package in an attempt to stave off a worsening of the crisis and jump-start a recovery, Democrats supported the measure by a vote of 211–44; Republicans voted 168–8 against it. There is again, as with judicial nominations, a general difference of opinion between the parties as to the best way to encourage investment and job growth; the typical Democrat and the typical Republican tend to bring different assumptions to the table. But even given those different starting points, is it likely that so many different individuals, from diverse backgrounds, experiences, and constituencies, would find such an incredible degree of uniformity if not for the imperative of maintaining party cohesion? With party leaders in the states holding power over the makeup of one's electoral district, party leaders in Congress controlling committee assignments and the party's purse strings, and partisan activists controlling party primaries, the pressure against exercising independent judgment is almost impossible to resist.

The lawmaking process isn't the only part of government in which the paralysis caused by partisanship can wreak great damage. The president of the United States is not the "head of government," but he is the head of a very large part of it, and the hundreds of executive branch departments and agencies over which he presides affect every aspect of our public life, from medical research (National Institutes of Health and Food and Drug Administration) to federal law enforcement (Justice Department, FBI, Drug Enforcement Administration), to national security (Department of Defense, Department of Homeland Security), to combating international sex trafficking (State Department), to ensuring that airplanes don't collide in midair (Federal Aviation Administration). When the Senate fails to act in a timely manner to evaluate and confirm the president's nominees to manage those agencies, the impact is felt both in the United States and overseas. Unfilled ambassadorships weaken our diplomatic ties and our ability to deal with international drug traffic, military basing rights, copyright protections, and trade agreements. Failure to confirm federal judges so damages the justice systems that chief justices of the Supreme Court routinely decry the inability of the federal courts to manage their caseloads (this is not merely a technical matter: when cases drag on, the rights of real human beings are affected).

Given these facts, one would imagine that members of the Senate would place a high priority on ensuring that all but the most controversial presidential nominees received timely consideration. But that's not the case. In June 2011 the *New York Times* reported on a study, conducted by law professor Anne Joseph O'Connell of the University of California at Berkeley, which found that while 86 percent of Reagan's executive appointments were confirmed and in place by the end of his first year in office, at the same point in Obama's presidency, nearly three decades later, only 64 percent of his nominees had been approved.[3] Often the holdup in the confirmation process is completely unrelated to the qualifications or philosophy of the person nominated but rather is part of a larger political battle. The *Times* article quoted Professor Paul Light of New York University, who complained that the confirmation delays have "enormous impact on the ability to faithfully execute the law. It tends to create a molasses-like paralysis inside the agencies as they consider rules and regulatory actions because they have nobody who really speaks with the full authority of the administration."

As Pietro Nivola of the Brookings Institution described the phenomenon at a 2009 conference at James Madison's Montpelier home, the United States is trending toward something closer to a parliamentary system of government, with more party discipline and more party unity. Nivola is not greatly disturbed by these trends, but he sees difficulties with policies enacted largely by a single dominant political party, suggesting that as they brush aside competing views, "they may prove unbalanced and unstable over time absent bipartisan ballast and 'buy-in.'" He also warns that "sustaining a sturdy and dependable foreign policy demands that, to a large extent, partisan politics stop at the water's edge." The pattern in recent years, however, has been quite the opposite: if one party dominates, it rams through its preferences and produces laws and policies that anger tens of millions of Americans; if neither party dominates, and conflict takes precedence over compromise, problems remain unsolved and grow worse, and frustration undermines the public's confidence in government.

America's founders gave us the vision of a government based on the mediated will of the governed, with far greater central authority than had existed under the earlier Articles of Confederation but with internal checks against threats to liberty. It was up to the generations that followed to seize on that vision and flesh it out, to give it meaning, to take the baton and pass it on to shape a government that would retain the founding values and yet meet the challenges of each succeeding century. Over the years, the nation grew westward, secession was blocked, slavery was ended, refugees were welcomed and America became more diverse, and women gained their proper rights as full citizens. But along the way, something else happened; no, not one something, several somethings—a perfect storm of social, cultural, and political changes that now threaten to overwhelm us.

Strong political disagreements did not suddenly come into being in the twentieth century. Alexander Hamilton, one of the most important of the nation's founders, a member of George Washington's Cabinet, died in a duel; the man who killed him was the vice president of the United States. The newspapers and pamphlets that made up the media of Washington's time tended toward a nastiness that would make today's talk shows look tame by comparison. Freedom of the press was born with John Peter Zenger's acquittal by a jury that agreed he had libeled a public official (the appointed governor of New York) but that there was enough truth in what he had written that he should be allowed to say it. It was an important victory—one of the most important trials in America's history—but one result was a journalism that buried public officials in invective. The issues America grappled with in its early generations so inflamed passions that when Abraham Lincoln won the Republican nomination for president, cries for secession began to bear fruit, leading to the Civil War.

As government grew larger and more expensive, and became involved in more aspects of private and public life, predictable disagreements emerged. Traditional news outlets, including radio and television, had lost their sharp edges, however, and journalism schools had begun to teach their students that their goal should be fair, objective, and politically neutral reporting, with opinion reserved for the editorial pages. But that would not last, as the divisions between conservatives and liberals grew sharper in the years during and following World War II, heightened by the tensions generated during the Cold War, civil rights battles, and a proliferation of new federal agencies that some saw as necessary and others saw as costly and intrusive.

Fighting to maintain profitability in a changing media economy, many news outlets now put a premium on controversy. A proliferation of narrow and partisan media outlets—talk radio, cable television, blogs, and tweets—magnifies the dissent and turns it to fury (to get booked as a guest on many of today's "discussion" shows, one must first pass a preinterview test to ensure that he or she is sufficiently conflict-oriented). In Congress, party leaders, Newt Gingrich more than others, changed the legislative focus from policy development to nonstop hyperpartisan politics. The political system that had worked for decades disappeared in a new world of heightened and unceasing acrimony. This is a new world, and the party-driven politics of the past century must disappear, too, if Americans are to regain a sense of common identity and work together to solve the problems of the twenty-first century.

Although there had always been sharp divisions over proposed policy, except during the Civil War Americans nonetheless tended to think of themselves as one people; "e pluribus unum"—one from many—had been adopted as the nation's official motto at the very beginning of the Republic, when it was incorporated into the Great Seal of the United States. Though over the years there was renewed attention to our diversity—in nationality, class, gender, race, religion, occupation, geography—for the most part, we thought of ourselves as a single people. Those who were outside the national circle in terms of law and custom—slaves (and later even free blacks) and women—were brought in. In his farewell address, stepping down after two terms as the nation's first president, George Washington issued an appeal for national unity as "the main pillar in the edifice of your real independence, the support of your tranquility at home, your peace abroad; of your safety; of your prosperity; of that very Liberty, which you so highly prize." Washington warned, as Professor Walter McDougall has noted, against "internal divisions born of personal ambition, faction, party . . ." Washington said he hoped his remarks would help to "moderate the fury of party spirit," one of several ways in which his sage advice has been ignored to our detriment.[4] On becoming the nation's third president, Thomas Jefferson said in his inaugural address, "We are all Federalists; we are all Republicans," the precursor to Barack Obama's later assertion that "there's not a liberal America and a conservative America; there's the United States of America." But while it was largely true in Jefferson's time, it was far from true when Obama said it. Polarization, centered in the bitter rivalry between advantage-seeking political parties, had, as the Founders feared, divided us. There had always been divisions—disunity—in politics, and that was true in Washington's time and in Jefferson's, as it is today—but they saw, and warned of, the dangers inherent in "faction" and "party" and in putting one's partisan allegiance ahead of the national interest—something that is the common coin of today's political realm.

To most of us in the United States, party-centric parliaments are simply a foreign way of doing things, irrelevant to any but scholars of government. But America's founders were well aware of parliamentary systems and they made a conscious effort to create something very different in their new nation, putting most of the nation's power in the hands of elected representatives, making the legislative branch of government fully independent of the executive, and requiring that all members of Congress actually live in the states they represent. That system is disappearing, as presidents and legislators who share the same party label increasingly see themselves as allies, not as independent actors, and party solidarity trumps both analysis and representation. Political parties are not inherently bad—citizens of common disposition will naturally seek each other out and combine to achieve agreed-upon ends—but when the pursuit of party power becomes the end goal and not merely a tool for achieving a better society, it is democracy itself that is laid beneath the guillotine's blade.

PART II

Reforming the Election System

THREE

Reclaiming Our Democracy

You must clear your mind of the fancy . . . that the institutions
under which we live are natural, like the weather. They are not. . . .
We take it for granted that they have always existed and must always exist. That is a dangerous mistake.
—GEORGE BERNARD SHAW

American democracy is a hybrid, and it is in that hybrid nature that
its success depends. Our system recognizes that we are by nature
both protective of independence and individuality, and committed
to community. It is our Constitution's recognition of, and respect
for, both facets of our nature that form the basis for how we govern
ourselves; it is why we operate collectively and honor singularity. It
is why our constitutional system both empowers and constrains the
government, which often, but not always, pursues policies that most
of us want. Despite the occasional complaints of those who wish the
United States were more thoroughly democratic—that is, that the
majority will would automatically translate into public law—citizens
retain considerable input into government decisions by virtue of
being able to select those who will ultimately decide. So long as our
laws remain within the bounds of the federal Constitution and are
judged to be meritorious by those men and women whom we elect
to Congress and the presidency, the voters' preferences will be re-

spected. Although majority rule is conditional, the right of the people to survey their communities and select from among their neighbors those who will write the laws is a key element of our democracy. This is the fundamental political value we project to the rest of the world, time and again—Woodrow Wilson reluctantly taking America to war "to make the world safe for democracy"; Ronald Reagan creating a National Endowment for Democracy to support development of democratic institutions in other nations; Barack Obama embracing the Arab Spring as a springboard to the expansion of democracy in the Middle East. How ironic, then, that we who hold ourselves out as exemplars—and promoters—of democracy have lost—in fact, have willingly surrendered—a central element of our own national democracy: that right of the people to freely choose from among all those men and women who may wish to offer themselves to us as public leaders.

Political theorists have often argued that political parties are essential ingredients of democracies, but here in the United States we are finding that the party system we have developed over the past century may instead pose a great threat to democracy. Of course, the United States is not a direct democracy—like Plato before them, this country's founders well understood the dangers of "mass rule" and therefore established a complex system of divided powers and constitutional constraints to protect the rights of the people—but we are also a democracy at the most basic level: we hold dear the right of the people to choose the nation's leaders and, if we don't like the decisions they make, to boot them out of office. It is that right—the power to choose from among our own number those who will make our laws—that is our most fundamental power-to-the-people right as Americans. It is what makes us citizens, not merely subjects of the state.

That right has been eroded.

In what way was it envisioned that we were to ensure that the voices of the people would actually be taken seriously in the councils of government? First, the framers wanted the people we elect to office actually to know us—to live among us and know firsthand our interests and concerns and preferences. They dealt with that part of the equation forthrightly in the Constitution: demonstrating their commitment to a government in which the citizens themselves hold ultimate power, they required in the very first article of the Constitution that all members of both the United States Senate and the House of Representatives actually be inhabitants of the states from which they were elected. It may have been possible to "represent" Manchester or Coventry or Leeds in the British Parliament and still be unable to locate any of those cities on a map, but that was not to be the case in America. In addition, as Edmund Burke argued, national legislators should function as more than mere rubber stamps for their constituents, whose knowledge or understanding of the issues may be limited. To be good legislators, they should not only be personally familiar with the needs and opinions of the electors but also apply their own understanding, experience, and judgment to the important issues confronting the entire nation, even if the national good conflicted with the wishes or concerns of their constituents. It's a two-way street: the elected legislator must know the people, but the people must also know their legislators. They must have the ability not only to select a neighbor but to choose from among their many neighbors the ones best suited by background, intelligence, thoughtfulness, energy, manner, persuasiveness, judgment, and so on to represent them adequately when laws were being made and policies established. This also means that a sufficient number of choices must actually be available to voters.

Step One: Take Away the Right of the Parties to Control Access to the Ballot

Under our current political party system, in which political parties—essentially, private power-seeking clubs—are permitted to narrow our choices, most voters, when they go to the polls for November's general elections, find that their only serious choices have effectively been reduced to Candidate A, the Democrat, and Candidate B, the Republican, both of whom had been deemed sufficiently loyal to their party's interests to win the endorsement of the activists in those respective clubs. Although the experience has been duplicated from one end of the country to the other, two examples from the 2010 U.S. Senate races will illustrate the point.

At that time, the state of Delaware had an estimated population of 843,524. In the Republican primary for the U.S. Senate seat that had been vacated by Vice President Joe Biden, Christine O'Donnell won a total of 30,561 votes, narrowly defeating veteran congressman (and former governor) Mike Castle. O'Donnell's vote total was less than 4 percent of the population of the state, and the combined total of the voters in that primary was just over 6 percent of the population. But when the state's voters went to the polls for the general election in November, Castle, who was still widely popular, was not one of the Senate choices available to them. Because parties choose their nominees, and the subsequent general-election campaigns are waged as a choice between the party nominees, the options available to Delaware's voters were severely curtailed. Slightly more than 6 percent of the citizens of Delaware determined the options available to the other 94 percent.

This circumstance highlights a specific and very undemocratic feature of modern American politics: both Castle and O'Donnell wanted to serve in the United States Senate, and both had large groups of supporters who believed them to be capable and representative of their views. If Castle had won the Republican primary, Delaware's voters would have then been denied the option of voting for O'Donnell. In the end, O'Donnell, as the Republican Party's nominee, lost the general election to Democrat Chris Coons, who had been the Middlesex County Executive. While Coons shows every sign of becoming a capable member of the Senate, we will never know whether he or Mike Castle would have ended up as the senator for Delaware's nearly one million citizens, because thirty thousand O'Donnell supporters denied them the opportunity to make that choice.

In 2010 the population of the state of Utah was 2,784,572, making it more than three times as populous as Delaware. It had long been served in the United States Senate by Robert Bennett (and by Bennett's father before him). In Utah, the selection of the Republican general-election candidate begins at a convention of party activists. That year, fewer than 2,000 convention delegates (out of a total of some 3,500) voted to nominate someone other than Bennett for the next Senate term; Bennett finished in third place and was therefore eliminated from the contest. As a result of the votes cast by just one one-thousandth of Utah's total population, Bennett was no longer available to the rest of the state's voters as a choice to represent them in the Senate. Because neither of the two candidates who divided the remainder of the convention vote, Tim Bridgewater and Mike Lee, won the required 60 percent of the convention delegates, they ran against each other in a similarly closed election, this time a primary. Lee defeated Bridgewater by a vote of 98,512 to 93,905. Now not only was Bennett, a longtime senator, no longer a possible choice for Utah voters, neither was Bridgewater, even though he had finished first at the convention and had narrowly lost the primary. With less than 45 percent of the convention vote and fewer than 100,000 primary votes, Mike Lee was able to keep both Bennett and Bridgewater off the general-election ballot and therefore unavailable as choices for the state's nearly three million citizens. Again, perhaps Lee will be a good United States senator, but we will never know if he would have been elected had Utah's voters been permitted to choose freely among all of their possible choices.

John Avlon, writing for CNN.com, cited the lesser known but

similar example of Adrian Fenty, the charismatic young mayor of Washington, DC, who had often been thought of as a younger Barack Obama.[1] Inheriting a city that had long been plagued by inadequate schools, Fenty had appointed an aggressive reformer, Michelle Rhee, as chancellor of public education. Rhee's work in upgrading the city's schools was featured in the acclaimed documentary *Waiting for Superman*. Fenty ran for reelection in 2010 and received the endorsement of the *Washington Post* for another term. But teachers' unions poured money into the closed Democratic primary, in which Fenty was challenged by City Councilman Vincent Gray, and despite a majority of city residents telling pollsters that the city had improved under Fenty's watch, they could not vote for his reelection because he lost the Democratic primary by a margin of 53–46 percent. (Fenty won the Republican primary as a write-in candidate but had previously promised Democratic voters that he would not accept a Republican nomination.) "Independent voters and Republicans . . . never had a chance to cast a ballot in this election for their mayor," Avlon wrote. "Instead the election was effectively over before the higher-turnout general election was ever held."

"The lesson: Closed partisan primaries are fundamentally unrepresentative," Avlon concluded. "They're too easily hijacked by ideological activists and party hacks beholden to special interests. And because these local primaries are the gauntlet that candidates have to run, they lead directly to the culture of hyperpartisanship that now threatens to paralyze our capacity for effective self-government. The parties have forgotten that they are not the purpose of our politics."

To be clear, the primary battles that ended the political careers of Robert Bennett, Mike Castle, and Adrian Fenty are not new phenomena. In 1978, Republican economist Jeffrey Bell, a member of the American Conservative Union's national board of directors, defeated a liberal Republican, Clifford Case, an incumbent United States

Senator, in a New Jersey party primary. Bell and Case together received nearly a quarter of a million votes. Bell then lost the general election to Democrat Bill Bradley, and New Jersey hasn't elected a Republican to the Senate since. Two years later, in 1980, a little-known conservative New York town official named Alfonse D'Amato defeated incumbent Senator Jacob Javits in a Republican primary, taking advantage of Javits's poor health and liberal voting record. Javits tried to retain his seat by running in the general election as an Independent (just as incumbent Joseph Lieberman later did in Connecticut after losing his Democratic primary), but he succeeded only in drawing votes from the Democratic nominee, Congresswoman Elizabeth Holtzman, thereby helping to ensure D'Amato's victory. Bell's narrow victory over Case (118,555 to 115,082) and Bradley's subsequent victory over Bell in the general election leave in doubt what the outcome might have been had Case, too, been on the ballot in November; perhaps he and Bell would have split the vote, as Javits and Holtzman did in New York, and Bradley would have won in any case, but we'll never know because voters were not given that choice.

In a bizarre example of the effect of highly ideological party primaries, in 2010 longtime Republican Senator Arlen Specter, convinced he would lose a primary to the more conservative Pat Toomey, switched parties and ran for reelection as a Democrat instead—only to lose in the Democratic primary to Congressman Joe Sestak, who lost to Toomey in November. Who would have won in Pennsylvania if Sestak, Toomey, and Specter had all been on the ballot? No one can say. The problem is not primaries—parties will continue to exist as long as people are allowed to associate freely, and they should be allowed to choose the candidate who will carry their flag in the ensuing general election; what they should not be allowed to do is prevent others from running.

University of Chicago Professor Geoffrey Stone has drawn a connection between congressional polarization and the party primary system that determines who will run for congressional seats. "Republicans and Democrats vote in separate primaries," he notes, resulting in one candidate who is the most popular among Republicans and one is who most popular among Democrats, both of whom are likely to be relatively far from the center. "As a consequence, candidates selected in party primaries usually do not reflect the views of the 40 to 45 percent of Americans in the moderate middle. Rather, they are more likely to represent the 30 percent on either end of the spectrum. That phenomenon appears to play a large role in producing the kind of polarization inherent in having two candidates whose views are fairly far apart."[2]

Exacerbating the current scenario, Stone told the American Academy of Arts and Sciences, "is the fact that participation in primary voting has fallen dramatically over the last half-century, from more than 70 percent fifty years ago to about 40 percent today. The people who are most likely to vote in party primaries are those who are most invested in the selection. They are likely to hold more extreme views than moderate voters."

Because most living Americans have grown up with this peculiar system—first the activists in our two major parties decide whom they will put forth for our major public offices, then we go to the polls in November to choose between the two options they present to us—we have assumed that this was the natural order of things. In fact, what we have today is not a legacy of 1789, when most of the new nation's leaders were fearful of political parties and the damage they could do, but an outdated relic of the late 1800s and early 1900s, when Progressives pushed for adoption of primary elections. By 1916, all but a handful of states had instituted the direct primary system under which a party candidate was selected by a public vote, rather than by party leaders in backroom deals. It was an important reform but a good example of the dangers of unintended consequences. The primaries and nominating conventions were open only to party members. This reform was supposed to give citizens a bigger role in the election process; instead, in an era of highly charged and confrontation-oriented media, sharp divisions over the direction of government, and the increased role of primary elections in selecting party nominees, the influence of party leaders has been supplanted by that of a subset of party activists who are often highly ideological and largely uninterested in finding the common ground necessary to govern a diverse nation of more than three hundred million people.

We Americans believe in choice. In almost every facet of our lives, from soups to soaps to stereos, we expect, and demand, multiple options. How strange it is that in the area that counts far more than any of these and that determines how much we will pay in taxes, what government services we will receive, and even whether our sons or daughters or husbands or wives or brothers or sisters will be sent off to fight and possibly die on a foreign battlefield, we allow two private organizations whose principal goal is the gaining and keeping of power (Republican and Democratic party leaders generally support their club's nominees, almost regardless of their political beliefs) to tell us that on election day we are allowed to choose between only the two people they have told us we must choose between.

In the election contest that resulted in my going to Congress as the representative of Oklahoma's Fifth Congressional District, I became the Republican nominee by winning a closed primary election against a man named G. T. Blankenship. I had never held any elective office or any other position of particular responsibility; I was unknown to most in my community, inexperienced, and clueless about the legislative process. In one of my first speeches on the House floor, I referred to Speaker Tip O'Neill as "your honor" instead of "Mr. Speaker" and then attempted to address the House from the wrong set of microphones. Blankenship, on the other hand, was a very successful businessman who had served as the Republican Party's leader in the Oklahoma legislature and then as the state's attorney general. I defeated him very narrowly (it took a recount to determine the winner). I hope I did a decent job of representing my constituents and serving the country for the next sixteen years, but G. T. Blankenship would have undoubtedly been a superb member of Congress. If he could have appeared on the general-election ballot, where all of Oklahoma's registered voters could have had the option of choosing him over me or the Democratic candidate that year, he very likely would have won and represented the state with great skill. I certainly would not have preferred that outcome, but I do prefer a political system in which the voters would have that choice.

It is not impossible for candidates who lose in a primary, or who run separately from the two major political parties as Independents or third-party candidates, to win a place on the general-election ballot, but it is very difficult. In 2006, Senator Joe Lieberman lost the Democratic Party primary to a more liberal and strongly antiwar challenger named Ned Lamont. Lieberman then ran successfully on a "Lieberman for Connecticut" ticket in the general election. But Lieberman's situation was unusual. Like Castle and Bennett, he was well known and already had a very strong base of popular support in the state (he had been a state legislator, the state's attorney general, a longtime senator, and, in 2000, his party's vice-presidential nominee). Connecticut is also one of only four states that do not prohibit a candidate from appearing on the ballot in the general election after losing a party primary. In the other forty-six states, so-called sore loser laws, designed to protect party dominance, either expressly ban an Independent campaign by a primary loser or have simultaneous filing deadlines that make it impossible to launch another election effort after the primary period has ended. After a massive and expensive effort, Lieberman was able to gather enough signatures to win a place on the November ballot under his own party label. To Lieberman's consternation, most of his Democratic colleagues in the Senate supported Lamont in the campaign, with loyalty to the party ticket trumping any other consideration, but Lieberman won reelection nonetheless. Even though Lamont was not the choice of Connecticut voters, given the relative weakness of the Republican Party in that state he might well have become their senator had Lieberman not defied tradition and staged his own Independent party campaign—and been in one of the few states that allowed it. In a truly democratic election system, sore loser laws would be repealed and ballot access expanded.

In Alaska, Senator Lisa Murkowski likewise lost a closed party primary, but, unlike Connecticut, Alaska's rules precluded her from appearing on the November ballot; instead she had to wage a write-in campaign. Given her built-in advantages (she had been in the Senate for eight years, and her father had been both a senator and a governor) she narrowly won after a protracted court fight that included challenges to ballots on which Alaska's voters had struggled to spell her name correctly. For candidates in most other states, those special twists would not be available. Lose to a small band of committed party loyalists and your candidacy is over, no matter how skilled, qualified, smart, or honest you might be, or how popular you are with the majority of your state's voters.

Several efforts have been made to remedy this thoroughly undemocratic process. A number of states, for example, have adopted an "open" election system that is essentially a party primary in which people who have not been party members previously may claim to identify with it on primary election day and thus participate in its "weeding-out" process. Such a primary is not truly open at all; it merely recognizes late joiners. There are several problems with this approach. The first is its interference with the right of free association and the ability of groups of like-minded people to make their own choice as to who will represent them (a right the Supreme Court has upheld). The second is that while somebody who was a Democrat yesterday may claim to be a Republican today in order to vote in the Republican primary, he cannot then also vote in the Democratic primary; he would gain the right to affect a campaign among one set of contestants but would give up the right to choose from within the second set of prospects. The third and most glaring failing is that this system may be used to pick not the best candidate but the worst. For example, a Republican may opt to vote in a Democratic primary for a candidate unlikely to win the general election, thereby helping the Republican candidate he really prefers; it's a clever stratagem but one designed to achieve party success, not good governance.

Another option, which has won the support of a number of frustrated voters, is the development of a third major political party. There are at least two significant weaknesses to this approach, which continues the damaging practice of using political parties as the foundational blocks of our democratic system. Parties exist to gain power. In the beginning, they are likely to seek power for the advancement of particular policies they define as essential to good government. Over time, however, two things can happen: first, they may find that winning and maintaining power is a sufficient end in itself, in which case the idea of working cooperatively with rivals for that power becomes decidedly unattractive. When party primacy becomes not a means but an end, a united front becomes essential and the number of issues on which unity is demanded grows far beyond the original agenda. The political parties that formed in the earliest days of the Republic (despite the warnings of George Washington, John Adams, Thomas Jefferson, and James Madison) were nothing like the parties that dominate American politics today. Their purposes were narrow—alliance with Great Britain or France, high tariffs or low tariffs. Today's parties, however, march in lock-step on issues large and small, from taxing to spending, trade policy to military policy, and to confirmation or rejection of executive branch nominees for ambassadorships, judgeships, cabinet secretaries, agency directors, and seats on the Supreme Court.

The second problem with a third party, in a system based on party identity and party cohesion, is that elections will often leave no single party with a majority in the legislature. Coalitions must be formed—voting blocs made up of multiple parties that commit themselves to working together. In such a case, parties with few members, few legislative seats, and policy positions well outside the mainstream gain inordinate power; they become a tail wagging the legislative dog because failing to meet their extreme demands can cause the entire coalition to collapse. If two parties, with their enforced unity and hardened agendas, have proven such a dramatic failure, think how much worse it would be if we simply added more of the same.

Some proposals would actually make the current system worse. Among the most heavily promoted are plans to create a system of "instant runoff voting," in which voters would rank candidates in order of preference. The votes received by a candidate who did not finish among the top two vote getters would automatically be reassigned to those voters' second choice. If the second choices were also eliminated, the votes would then go to the voters' third choice, and so on, all of this tabulating and tracking being done by computer. The goal, apparently, is to bypass the need to have actual runoff elections in which the two candidates with the most votes—if neither received more than 50 percent—would face off against each other, with the voters then able to concentrate their attention on the merits and performance of the two. Bypassing a real runoff would certainly be cheaper. But as anybody who has lived in a state with runoff elections can attest, it is not uncommon for the candidate who finished second in the first round to win in the runoff precisely because the supporters of every eliminated candidate had already chosen not to back the front-runner, and the two-person race gave voters the opportunity to compare the two finalists side by side in a way they could not have done when the field was more crowded—a far more important consideration than saving the cost of a runoff election.

The abundance of proposed reforms, good and bad alike, makes clear how desperate citizens are for something different from the current primary systems, which empower small numbers of hard-core partisans to hijack our elections. Here are some better ways to break away from the outdated system that lies at the core of our political dysfunction.

Eliminate the ability of political parties to determine who can run in a general election. We must break the power of partisans to keep candidates off the general-election ballot by creating new systems of open integrated primaries. Three states have now made that leap into a better and more democratic future. Louisiana did it several years ago and, after a brief return to the kind of party-based system that is common in other states, went back to the non-party-based primaries. Washington State did the same in 2006. California followed in 2010. In those states every candidate for a particular office, regardless of party—Republican, Democrat, Green, Libertarian, etc.—appears on the same ballot, and every registered voter in the state may participate in the selection process. In the end, the top two finishers run against each other in a general election, even if both are from the same party, and even if neither is from one of the two major political parties. Normal ballot access rules apply (for example, requiring a certain number of petition signatures or payment of a predetermined filing fee or some other method to deter frivolous candidates), but then all of the state's voters may choose from among all of the possible options. Party activists can anoint their favored candidates and give them whatever support they can muster, but they can no longer determine whose names may appear on the ballot. The people have a much wider range of options, and they, not private power-seeking clubs, control these states' elections.

Some have complained that depriving party activists of the power to limit voters' choices would encourage hundreds of candidates to run in every election, making it impossible for citizens to make sense of the ensuing noise and confusion. But that presupposes that states would do away with all their other procedures for screening out less serious candidates. States have, or can easily create, measures to weed out cranks and conspiracy theorists, including a requirement that candidates gather nominating signatures from a predetermined number of registered voters to become eligible for inclusion on the ballot. Compiling reports from *Ballot Access News*, the Center for Range Voting found that, from the time that preprinted ballots were first used in around 1890 until 2005, only twice did a ballot for a statewide office in the United States list more than ten candidates, "provided at least 2,500 signatures were required to qualify."[3]

Some also argue that a system without partisan nominees would take away important "cues" that enable voters to make informed decisions. For example, if a ballot contains the name of only one Republican and one Democrat (and perhaps one or two minor-party candidates), voters who align themselves with one of those parties will know which candidate for whom to cast their vote. This argument amounts to the insultingly undemocratic theory that Americans are not smart enough to know how to vote without being positioned under flashing signs that proclaim "This is the one you want." The most egregious example of this mind-set came in the early years of the Obama administration, when the Justice Department intervened to overturn a referendum in the small town of Kinston, North Carolina, where voters had decided to join most of the state's other communities in conducting nonpartisan local elections. The Justice Department concluded that the community's African-American population would need to know which candidates were Democrats in order to have the necessary information for casting their vote.

In a system of open integrated primaries, there might actually be three or four Republicans on the ballot, as well as that many Democrats, Independents, Green Party candidates, and Libertarians. Or perhaps candidates would simply run under only their own names, relying on the information they had made public about their qualifications and policy positions. Who would tell the people who they are supposed to vote for?

That the argument used by the Justice Department in Kinston is offensive and insulting is not the only reason the usefulness of cues has been outlived. If such cues were necessary at some point in our history, when communications systems were more limited and education was less widespread, that time is long past. The cue is a political dinosaur, an outdated relic of an earlier time. Today, candidates have multiple forums to reach voters and to explain what they would propose to do if elected. More important, any voter who wants to find out about a candidate's background and policies has ample opportunity to do so. Today, consumers receive bills in the mail with messages on the return envelope such as "Don't have a stamp? Pay online." In a world in which companies assume you are more likely to have a computer than a postage stamp, finding out how a particular congressional candidate feels about foreign aid is not difficult. Cues are helpful in a parliamentary system, where a voter may be concerned primarily with choosing whichever candidate will most loyally follow orders from party leaders, but are of little use in a system like ours, in which elected officials are presumed to think for themselves and to be mindful of the interests of the particular constituencies that have elected them.

Even if party-specific primaries were eliminated, political parties would continue to exist because people of similar opinions tend to coalesce to advance their preferred policies. Nothing would prevent those groups from endorsing candidates and making those endorsements known to the electorate. My purpose is not to silence partisan voices but rather to take away the parties' ability to silence the voices of those who are not the choice of party insiders and activists.

An election—the choosing of our leaders—is the single most fundamental element in a democratic system of government. Yet our state and local governments have abdicated their responsibilities to oversee the election process. Not only have they turned the job over to political parties, but they take money from taxpayers to pay for these party functions. Because primaries and conventions are now dominated by activists who demand loyalty and see compromise as selling out, candidates who seek to be on the November ballot find themselves under great pressure to take hard-line positions. This tendency toward rigidity—and the party system that enables it—is at the root of today's political dysfunction.

More and more, voters are opting out of that system. As we've already seen, in Massachusetts, where the Republican Scott Brown won the seat previously held by Democrat Edward Kennedy, a plurality of voters are not Democrats or Republicans but "unenrolled." In most states, however, the only option available to this growing number of Independent voters is either to pretend to be party members (in which case they can vote in one primary but not both) or to wait until the general election and then choose between the two candidates they are allowed to consider.

A political system in which voters have maximum choice will not necessarily elect more moderate or centrist officials, and centrism itself should not be the goal: many important democratic advances, including legislation prohibiting discrimination against women and African-Americans, were the result of political movements that were not, at the time, centrist. But when all of a state's voters, rather than merely its activists, have a voice in determining the results of the election process, there is a far greater chance that the winners will be candidates who are more willing to accept compromise as a necessary ingredient of government. And candidates from third or fourth parties will have a better chance of finishing in the top two in a completely open primary than they would on a general-election ballot designed to pit the designated champions of the two major parties against each other. This will be even more likely if all candidates, regardless of party, have an increased opportunity to get their message to the voting public.

The use of party primaries to limit voter choice has had a long and sordid history. In 1921, in *Newberry v. United States*, the Supreme Court ruled that the Congress lacks the authority to regulate primaries or other nomination procedures, essentially concluding that political parties are private organizations. Justice James C. Mc-Reynolds, writing for the Court, argued that a primary, which simply chose the nominee of one party, was not the same as an actual election. However, two separate facts merged to give a disturbing meaning to this nuanced decision. First, overt racial discrimination was then pervasive throughout the United States, especially in the South; and second, with no meaningful two-party system in the South or in many machine-dominated cities, simply winning the Democratic Party nomination was, despite McReynolds's claim, a virtual guarantee of victory in November. Excluding people from participating in the Democratic primary was tantamount to silencing their political voices, at least in terms of the electoral process. Seeing an opportunity, two years later members of the Texas legislature took advantage of the *Newberry* ruling by enacting a new state law that expressly prohibited blacks—most of whom were Republicans—from voting in primaries on the assumption that the courts would not interfere with the rules for these "private" party activities. In 1935, in *Grovey v. Townsend*, the Supreme Court again found that primaries were private affairs and that blacks had no constitutional right to participate. Not until 1944, in *Smith v. Allwright,* did the Court reverse course and declare that because Texas state laws had made primaries an integral part of the electoral process, excluding blacks from participation violated the equal protection clause of the Fourteenth Amendment. The number of blacks registered to vote in Texas swelled from thirty thousand in 1940 to one hundred thousand seven years later.

The Court had finally gotten it right. The political parties are indeed private clubs, but in most states their procedures—sanctioned and often paid for by the taxpayers—can skew the outcomes of general elections and shape the makeup of the decidedly nonprivate institutions that make and enforce our nation's laws. It is essential that the laws be changed to ensure that, in this most critical ingredient of a democratic political system, meaningful participation is expanded and voter choices are multiplied. Whether it's exercised for purposes of racial discrimination or simply to win a partisan advantage, the stranglehold of parties on the political process must be ended. The mere act of establishing an open and integrated primary system would break the partisan and ideological chokehold on the general-election ballot and create a much truer system of democratic self-government. Members of Congress would have more freedom to base their legislative decisions on their constituents' concerns and their independent evaluations of a proposal's merits. They would represent us, not their political clubs.

Other changes could make the elections process even more representative. One option, favored by congressional scholar Norman Ornstein of the American Enterprise Institute, would be to adopt a system of mandatory voting similar to those used in several other countries. Responding to a list of reform proposals offered by Tennessee Congressman Jim Cooper, Ornstein noted that Australia fines nonvoters the equivalent of $15 to $20 and that election-day turnout, as a result, "hovers around 97 percent."[4] It's uncertain how well Americans would take to being compelled to vote, even though similar requirements exist for other civic participation, including making oneself available for jury duty. Some people have questioned whether government would actually be improved if mandatory voting caused much greater participation by the uninformed and uninterested, but Ornstein argues that simply increasing turnout would force candidates to reframe their messages to appeal to a broader cross section of the constituency and reduce the power of the more extreme voters who dominate smaller-turnout elections.

Another approach is to remove the existing institutional barriers to voting for those who might care about the issues and be informed about the policy options offered by the various candidates, but who find it difficult to participate because of outdated election laws that generally require voters to cast their ballots near their homes during daylight hours on a Tuesday. While those requirements may have been reasonable enough half a century ago (voting in one's own home precinct ensured that campaign workers could check the voter rolls to verify a would-be voter's registration), the computerization of registration data allows the same verification capacity practically anywhere. For the professional, the self-employed, the stay-at-home, the highly mobile, and the worker with flexibility, voting during a midweek workday poses little problem. For a factory worker or a nonmanagement employee, however, finding time to leave work to vote, even in a nearby polling place, may be difficult. And there is no longer any valid basis for such impediments to participation. Making election day a national holiday (in midweek, so the day off would not morph into a long weekend and tempt voters to load the kids into the car and head off for Six Flags) is one possible solution. Keeping polling places open until 10 pm would also help; the only reason for closing the polls earlier is to enable the news media to have results on the evening television news or in the morning newspapers, but a desire for higher viewership or reader-ship is not a sufficient reason to make it more difficult to exercise one's constitutional right to vote. The goal is to make it easier, not harder, for citizens to take part in the essential freedom of a demo-cratic society.

By creating an open primary, with its greater number of candi-dates to choose between, and simultaneously making it easier for prospective voters to cast their ballots, we would take a major step forward toward ensuring that the "democracy" part of our national governing system is much more of a reality.

The system we now have, in which power-seeking private clubs choke off our political options, is ordained by neither the Constitu-tion nor common sense. State and local governments have not only abdicated their responsibility to oversee America's election process and turned the job over to political parties, they take money from taxpayers to pay for these party functions. We are being taxed for the privilege of reducing our own choices as to who will represent us in making the nation's laws. We must reclaim the democratic right to choose among our neighbors the candidates we believe would best represent us in the councils of government.

FOUR

Drawing a Line in the Sand

We are in the business of rigging elections.
—NORTH CAROLINA STATE SENATOR MARK McDANIEL
(quoted in the *New Yorker*)

Step Two: Take Away the Parties' Control over Redistricting

The democratic principle of choice in the selection of one's leaders has a corollary. As pointed out earlier, the authors of America's Constitution insisted that a legislator representing Rhode Island be an actual inhabitant of Rhode Island, not just somebody who had once passed through, or had once lived there, or had a business relationship with a Rhode Island resident. If you live in the state, you presumably know something of its patterns, its economics, its culture. In the case of Rhode Island, you might understand the importance of the maritime industry and be familiar with the state's particular role as a champion of religious liberty or with the importance of the interstate highway system (even though, in Rhode Island's case, that system largely consists of Interstate 95). You might understand Burke's admonition to use your own intellect and judgment in making policy decisions, but you also know that you are Rhode Island's voice in national deliberations and it is up to you to take its needs and preferences seriously. The voters of Rhode Island have chosen one of their neighbors—you—to go to Washington on their behalf. Nothing in the Constitution is more fundamental to the idea that the people are not subjects but citizens: this land is our land, to paraphrase the song, but more specifically, we are in charge and responsible for our own national destiny.

So how does that important principle work if congressional district boundaries are drawn on the basis of one's party registration, while other commonalities are ignored? What if the controlling factor is not common interest but party advantage?

Gerrymandering—shaping congressional districts for partisan advantage—has been a part of American political culture since 1812, when Elbridge Gerry, then the governor of Massachusetts, oversaw the drafting of peculiarly shaped state senate districts to produce election results beneficial to his own political party (the name *gerrymander* was coined to describe one exceptionally odd-shaped district that some thought looked like a salamander). It is a practice that continues to this day. The Twelfth Congressional District in North Carolina snakes up Interstate 85 from south of Charlotte to north of Winston-Salem, eighty-three narrow miles from southwest to northeast. California's Twenty-third District hugs 132 miles of the Pacific coast in a narrow strip from south of Oxnard to north of San Luis Obispo. Texas's Twenty-second District, the home of former House Majority Leader Tom DeLay, sprawls to the south of Houston in a shape vaguely reminiscent of a submachine gun. Several districts look like barbells, with a long strip barely wider than a highway connecting two bulbous population centers.

The problem, of course, is not the offense to artistic sensibilities but the offense to the democratic idea that our elected officials should know us and our concerns. As Tennessee Congressman Jim Cooper wrote in *Boston Review*, "Each party is working hard to create fewer competitive districts. Advanced digital mapping and statistical analysis help them etch tiny lines on large and detailed maps, enabling them to split neighborhoods and blocks—because politicians know a great deal about your voting habits. The secret ballot is almost gone."[1] Cooper noted that in most states, the public is excluded from redistricting deliberations, even though "this secret election can determine the outcome of most congressional elections for the next ten years, possibly for generations."

This process affects Congress's ability to find common ground on important national issues. "Because relatively few centrists or independent voters participate in primaries," Cooper says, "newly elected extremists are vulnerable only to someone more extreme. . . . With a firm grip on their districts and no worries about alienating voters in the other party, gerrymandered extremists are often the loudest voices in Congress."

A redistricting strategy developed for party advantage ignited a particularly heated battle in Maryland in 2011 after Governor Martin O'Malley designed a new map that apportioned populous Montgomery County's racial minorities, which form the majority of the population in that county, into three separate congressional districts. Supporters of the plan openly boasted that it would help their party defeat longtime Republican incumbent Roscoe Bartlett and give their party control of seven of the state's eight congressional seats. Members of Maryland's Legislative Black Caucus argued that by redistributing the minority population in this way, the governor's plan would result in three districts in which, as critics told the *Washington Post*, only whites would be elected "for years to come."[2] Democratic State Senator C. Anthony Muse, a pastor and an African-American, claimed the plan "put the good of the party over the good of the people" and would "reward" minority voters for their support of the party "by diluting their political power." Senator Jamie Raskin, another Democrat, supported the plan as a necessary defense against Republican-led redistricting in other states. "This is not a Maryland problem with redistricting and gerrymandering," he said. "It's an American problem. All across America, people are complaining about extremely spliced and diced, curvy swervy districts where elected officials choose voters before voters choose elected officials."

Muse's concern—that party interests were superseding those of the people—echoed a common complaint. In Texas, for example, a federal court intervened in 2011 to block a redistricting plan that had been drawn up by the Republican majority in the Texas legislature. In the preceding decade, the state's population had soared by 21 percent, to more than twenty-five million, giving Texas four additional congressional seats. During this time the state's Hispanic population grew by 2.8 million and the African-American population by more than 500,000, compared with a growth of 465,000 in the white population. The court ruled that the Texas legislators had failed to adequately take into account the growth in the state's minority populations and substituted a new redistricting plan of its own, which would ensure that members of those minority groups would make up a majority of the voters in three of the new congressional districts. Texas Attorney General Greg Abbott urged the court to stay implementation of its plan but the court refused, leading Abbott to accuse it of "undermining the democratic process."[3] The U.S. Supreme Court ruled that the lower court had substituted too much of its own judgment for that of the legislature and sent the case back again, the continuing struggle reflecting the high stakes involved in a redistricting that could ultimately have a serious impact on which federal policies are enacted.

Policy outcomes may also be affected by whether incumbents run in "safe" or in competitive districts. In a district where any member of one's party is almost certain to win, a Republican incumbent's only real concern is a challenge from the right, and a Democrat's only fear is a challenge from the left; to the extent that one sticks to the positions advocated by partisan activists, there is little need to fear defeat and little need to be overly concerned with the presumably less ideological interests of the majority of the district's voters.

I am an example of how putting party first can undermine the citizens' right to be represented by somebody who understands their concerns. In 1976, I became the first Republican elected to Congress from my Oklahoma district in forty-eight years. Nearly three-quarters of the district's voters were Democrats, yet I easily won my next two races. The Democrats who controlled the state legislature were pessimistic about recapturing the seat and used their majorities to redraw the district's borders. Whereas I had previously represented a single large urban county (much of Oklahoma City and some suburbs) in the center of the state, my new district stretched north all the way to the Kansas border and east nearly to Arkansas in a huge upside-down "L." The goal was to put as many as possible of my fellow Republicans into my district in order to make the neighboring districts, from which these Republicans had been removed, safer for Democrats. I had grown up and gone to public schools in Oklahoma City, worked in newspapers and advertising agencies in Oklahoma City, been active in community organizations and party politics in Oklahoma City. I had worked to raise money to save the city's struggling symphony orchestra and for local organizations that provided assistance to starving children in Africa; I knew the city and felt comfortable representing its people. They were, as the Constitution envisioned, my neighbors. But my new district was much more rural, embracing five new counties filled with small towns, wheat farms, and cattle ranches. I knew few people in these counties, had never worked with them on any matters of common interest, and had rarely even passed through their towns or seen their farmlands. Rather than being represented by a member of their own community, familiar with their concerns, these tens of thousands of voters were thereafter to be "represented" by a congressman unfamiliar with the issues on which their liveli-hoods depended. And the urban and diverse communities I had rep-resented in Oklahoma City were now to be served by a congressman whose time and attention were shared, and whose policy positions were influenced, by a very different constituency. Community inter-ests had been subordinated to the interests of a political party that simply wanted to accumulate more power.

It would be easy to consider an example like this only in terms of its impact on a particular constituency or legislator. But the effects are more serious and far-reaching. Consider the well-known case of a gerrymandering campaign that significantly affected national pol-icy. From 1972 to 1982, Republican candidates for Congress in California received nearly as many votes in total as Democratic can-didates; not surprisingly, the state's congressional delegation in 1980 reflected that division—22 Democrats and 21 Republicans. In 1980, however, Republicans had succeeded in electing Ronald Reagan to the White House, and Democrats, fearful that Reagan would roll back the new federal programs they had created, were determined to weaken even further the Republican minority in the House of Rep-resentatives. A large part of that task fell to Representative Philip Burton, a California Democrat who took on the leadership of the state's redistricting effort. Even those whose political goals were set back by Burton's designs acknowledge the great skill he applied to the project. Large minority communities, which generally voted for Democratic candidates, were split; instead of piling up large majori-ties in one district, they were instead able to help Democrats win by comfortable but narrower majorities in several districts. Republican-leaning voters, on the other hand, were compressed into single dis-tricts that created safe seats for some but fewer Republican victories overall. Where those tactics did not work, district lines were twisted into strange configurations to maximize Democrats' chances for victory. In 1982, following the Burton redistricting, Democrats increased their margin in the delegation to 27–18, including capturing both of California's new seats—a gain of nine Democratic votes with which to contest the Reagan agenda, not because California voters had become more liberal but because party control of redistricting was focused on party advantage, not constituent representation.

The Burton redistricting plan used every known gerrymandering technique. It "cracked" districts open and spread voters into areas where their numbers could be used to maximum effect; it "stacked" Republicans into fewer districts so their collective impact would be lessened (a candidate who wins 80 percent of the vote instead of 51 percent still gets only one vote in Congress), and it drew snakes and salamanders and barbells to create a district map friendly to the Democratic Party. Incumbents became safer from challenge (thus reducing the necessity of being responsive to voter concerns), and congressional districts became less competitive.

Republicans have proven themselves no less skilled at mapmaking, as they demonstrated when House Republican Whip Tom DeLay orchestrated a special redistricting of his home state of Texas. DeLay pushed his redistricting plan through the Texas legislature in 2003, even though the district lines had already been redrawn in 2001 following the 2000 national census. In the meantime, however, Republicans had taken control of the Texas legislature, and DeLay saw an opportunity to gain a significant Republican advantage in Congress. Rather than waiting until after the 2010 census, as would be the custom, DeLay decided to strike quickly. The result was a significant change in the makeup of Congress. After the 2002 elections, based on the 2001 redistricting, the Texas House delegation consisted of 17 Democrats and 15 Republicans; after the 2004 elections, which used the new lines drawn by DeLay, Republicans had a 21–11 margin, providing the House Republicans with six additional votes while Democrats lost six.

The results of such partisan redistricting schemes can be destructive to representative democracy. Voter turnout may decline as citizens come to understand that their votes will not make much difference, and, with less competitiveness in the general election, candidates begin to worry more about pleasing the ideological activists who vote in primaries. The entire political process moves toward extreme and uncompromising positions.

How is it that the United States, the worldwide role model for representative self-government, has created a system in which "representation" is the last thing on the minds of those who shape our congressional districts? Part of the answer is that we have ceded responsibility for drawing our legislative districts to state legislatures in which the majority party can draw the lines pretty much as it wishes so long as it meets certain parameters such as contiguity, roughly equal populations, and no obvious discrimination against minorities. This great legislative power, wielded in some form in thirty-seven of the fifty states, explains why political observers often speculate on future Republican or Democratic gains in Congress based on how many state legislative majorities each party controls. When citizens vote for a member of the state house of representatives or state senate, or for governor, usually on the basis of local issues and concerns, they may have little awareness that they are also casting a vote on the future of national policy decisions—a twist possible only in a political system that allows congressional district lines to be drawn for party advantage.

There are other consequences as well. In a competitive district, a congressional candidate who appeals to a broad cross section of the electorate has a distinct advantage in a general election. But in districts that are heavily Republican or heavily Democratic, with no real opportunity for a candidate of another party to win, the incentives are often quite different: whoever emerges as winner of the party primary is almost guaranteed victory. As a result, candidates are under great pressure to align their policies with those of the more partisan, and more ideological, activists who tend to dominate those primaries; they become more independent of the voters who may actually be in a majority in the district and less independent of the uncompromising hardliners.

When I was growing up in Oklahoma, which was then as heavily Democratic as it is now Republican, political observers routinely referred to a win in a Democratic primary as "tantamount to victory" since Republicans could offer no meaningful opposition. The same result has been achieved in state after state through the drawing of congressional districts in which one party or the other is at an almost insurmountable disadvantage. In California, after voters took redistricting decisions out of the hands of partisans in the state legislature, a number of veteran members of Congress, suddenly faced with truly competitive districts, announced their retirement.

Those who concern themselves with redistricting commonly cite one of three goals. One is to provide competitiveness, to ensure that members of Congress and state legislators can be held accountable for their actions. Get too far out of sync with public sentiment, they argue, and disaffected voters can put you out of office. A second goal is that representatives be, well, representative. Communities have commonalities of interest, and the men and women elected to Congress should provide a voice for those common concerns. This implies a certain coherence to each district. The third goal cited by some is to provide for a "moderate" or "centrist" national legislature. In a diverse nation of 320 million people, it is vital to elect decision makers who are willing to seek common ground. Drawing district boundaries to favor the hard-line activists who vote in primaries has the effect of drawing lines in the sand; the winning candidates arrive in Washington prepared to do battle not for the common interest but for a partisan and ideological agenda.

Each of these positions has dedicated advocates who vigorously champion one goal as more important to the democratic process than the others. Amazingly, by ceding control of redistricting to the political parties, which act through their legislative majorities to achieve an altogether different goal—partisan advantage—all three of these good governance goals are erased. Party control of redistricting manages somehow to produce unrepresentative, uncompetitive, and ideologically inflexible outcomes simultaneously.

In addition to simple party interests, gerrymandering can be used to provide an advantage to communities that share noneconomic commonalities, an important example being the creation of majority-minority districts. These are congressional districts shaped to ensure that their minority constituents (generally African-American or Hispanic), traditionally underrepresented in the public deliberations, will have a greater chance of electing one of their own number. Interestingly, this practice has led to conflicts between Democratic Party activists and minority constituents who had generally supported them. In the most common examples, African-Americans cheered outcomes that would finally give them a place at the table, while party activists feared that the resulting district lines, by concentrating minority voters in a single district, would turn neighboring districts more conservative and Republican, and ultimately give the Republicans more seats. Clearly drawing district lines to produce preferred outcomes can create difficulties—and divisions—even within traditional voting blocs.

There is yet another questionable feature of the redistricting system. The democratic ideal is to allow voters to select candidates, but partisan redistricting can produce the opposite result, allowing candidates to select their voters. Potential candidates can carefully review the voting patterns of various neighborhoods or counties to determine how best to shape a district to give themselves a clear electoral advantage. Incumbents who have significant influence with state legislators can push to get districts drawn that will provide them with a constituency that will all but guarantee their reelection. State legislators with ambitions to run for Congress can do likewise, mapping out a district to their advantage: candidates choose their voters instead of the other way around.

Finally, partisan redistricting has yet another downside. Political scientists Danny Hayes and Seth McKee have found that redistricting can drive down participation in congressional elections and that the drop-off is most noticeable among African-Americans who have been shoved into new congressional districts with unfamiliar candidates. Following their study of eleven postredistricting elections in five states from 1992 through 2006, the authors found "a previously hidden effect of redistricting: it can widen the existing participation gap between Whites and Blacks in U.S. congressional elections."[4] Redistricting, they concluded, "is likely to disproportionately disadvantage" voters who are economically less well off. Conversely, if African-American voters were redistricted into constituencies that already had an African-American member of Congress, their voting participation rates were likely to increase. It is easy to see how party activists, if they controlled the shape of congressional districts, might take advantage of this fact to deliberately draw districts to either increase or decrease African-American turnout. This is one more way for candidates to select their voters instead of the other way around, and to put party interests first among redistricting priorities.

So fundamental is the concept of representativeness to American democracy that three of New York State's best-known United States Senators—Hillary Clinton, a native of Illinois and later a resident of Arkansas; Robert F. Kennedy, from Massachusetts; and James Buckley, from Connecticut—all had to move to New York before being elected. Clinton made a well-publicized statewide "listening tour" to become acquainted with the state's citizens and their concerns in advance of the election, even though she was already a well-known public figure nationally, as was Kennedy, a younger brother of a slain president and a former attorney general of the United States.

On the other hand, when Harold Ford, Jr., a former congressman from Tennessee who had moved to Manhattan to work in the financial industry, sought to run for the U.S. Senate in 2010, he drew sharp criticism for his lack of familiarity with any part of New York beyond Manhattan and quickly withdrew from the race. A congressman named Ed Foreman represented first western Texas and then southern New Mexico in the United States House of Representatives, but he had to move from one state to the other to be eligible to serve. None of these moves would have been necessary if the Constitution did not clearly require that representatives in Congress be familiar with the people they hope to serve by living in the state or district they represent. This is more than a simple technicality; it is a factor in what George Mason University Professor Hugh Heclo might label an "institutional responsibility."

How, then, do we ensure that congressional districts meet the legitimate goals a truly democratic government requires? By removing the power of state legislatures and governors to determine congressional district lines.

Brookings Institution scholar William Galston, speaking at a conference at James Madison's Montpelier home (where his colleague Pietro Nivola earlier had described America's drift toward a European-style parliamentary government), noted that "few western democracies draw up their parliamentary districts in so patently politicized a fashion as do U.S. state legislatures."[5] By Galston's reckoning, at least 10 percent, and maybe more than one-third of the reduction in competitive congressional districts over the past three decades, is the result of gerrymandering by state lawmakers aiming for party advantage. In thirteen states, however, the drawing of congressional district lines is left to nonpartisan or bipartisan panels that are either entirely or partially independent of the state legislature in the initial drawing of proposed district lines. The method of selecting panel members—and the extent to which their decisions are final—vary from state to state. Some require final approval from the state legislature, which will be under considerable public pressure to go along; some include legislators on the panels but require that the panels contain equal numbers of Republicans and Democrats.

Like most major reforms, fixing the redistricting process will require careful planning. Each state will have to develop its own system to ensure that members of redistricting commissions do not simply bring their own biases to the task, and that they have sufficient clout to ensure that their decisions are not ignored. Both dilemmas were highlighted in Arizona in 2011, when Governor Jan Brewer exercised her authority to impeach the head of that state's independent redistricting commission for what she characterized as "gross misconduct in office," which prompted a reporter for *USA Today* to note that her action "raises the question of whether Arizona or any other state can completely remove politics from redistricting."[6] The article described Arizona's redistricting commission law, in place for more than a decade, as "what had been a model of independent electoral mapmaking." For her part, the governor accused the commission of "putting a priority on making congressional districts competitive" rather than representative. Brewer's spokesman, Matthew Benson, said the governor "had to act" because the commission's draft maps had attempted to skew election results by increasing the number of districts along the state's border with Mexico, combining urban and rural areas, and unnecessarily cutting two counties in half. "Independent does not mean without oversight," he said. Democrats called Brewer's action "a breathtaking abuse of power" and described her move as part of a long "campaign of intimidation and interference." At almost the same time, in California, which had adopted its own form of nonpartisan redistricting in 2010, the state Supreme Court dismissed a Republican attempt to throw out the state commission's proposed redistricting plan.

As the battles in Arizona and California demonstrate, state lawmakers—whether as elected legislators or as ordinary citizens using the referendum or initiative process—will have to design their systems to protect against both commission bias and partisan interference. If their plans are drawn well, the resulting electoral maps will favor true voter choice rather than merely reflecting the outcome of pitched partisan battle. Despite the controversy in Arizona, Keesha Gaskins of New York University's Brennan Center for Justice described the state's commission process as a success, whether or not its proposed maps were adopted, because such commissions make public what has traditionally been a backroom process. There will inevitably be controversy over redistricting plans because both "representativeness" and "competitiveness" are valid concerns, as are attempts to give minorities a place at the table in congressional deliberations. The value of independent, nonpartisan redistricting commissions is that those competing values will be balanced on the basis of principle, not according to how they help one political party gain an electoral advantage. As Americans for Redistricting Reform notes on its website, independent redistricting commissions allow voters to choose their representatives, not the other way around.

FIVE

The Money Stream

Step Three: Reduce Spending, Increase Competition

Tennessee Congressman Jim Cooper, citing the more than $8.5 million spent on the most expensive U.S. House races, and the $27 million spent on the costliest Senate races, has called a new congressperson's identifying lapel pin "the most expensive piece of jewelry in the world."[1] He's right: political campaigns in the U.S. have become outrageously expensive.

But the amounts we spend on elections, and the time candidates spend fund-raising, should not be our only concerns. As opponents of campaign finance reform proposals have pointed out repeatedly, we Americans spend, collectively, less on congressional elections than we spend on snacks. Elections are certainly far more important (though often less satisfying) than potato chips. And if citizens were to spend more on the selection of qualified leaders than they spend on candy or text-messaging, that might well be a sign of a healthy, not a sick, democracy. So what's the problem?

This book deals with the role the political parties play in our election system and the translation of that influence into a governing system that precludes civility and compromise and makes it extremely difficult to deal effectively with important national issues. So some of the specific concerns about corporate and union funding, "bundling" of campaign contributions, political action committees (PACs), and now so-called super-PACs would seem at first glance to fall outside the scope of the argument. But no attempt at reforming American politics can be successful unless the funding of campaigns is made more equitable. Super-PACs enable money to be funneled into campaigns in unlimited amounts and with no means of identifying the contributors. Corporations may use their corporate treasuries to support political candidates based at least in part on the fiction that corporations are, legally, "persons" even though the very act of incorporation itself, which grants individuals acting within corporations legal immunities that are not otherwise available to "persons," is a clear acknowledgment that corporations are *not* people; the same Supreme Court decision (*Citizens United v. Federal Election Commission*) also allows labor organizations to use their funds in support of candidates even though many of the men and women whose dues help make up that funding pool did not voluntarily choose to join a union but are required to pay into the union treasury in order to keep their jobs. Suffice it to say that we would be well served by a law mandating that, for the purposes of campaign contributions, the term "persons" refers only to actual individual living human beings—no corporate money, no union money, no money from political action committees, no money from political parties. Political campaigns should be paid for by people, and only by people.

Campaign finance laws permit political parties, and thus party leaders, to play significant, often decisive roles in congressional races, helping to create a Congress in which legislators not only feel a strong sense of obligation to party leaders but are aware that their future success may depend on not alienating these leaders. Whereas an individual supporter is limited to a $2,500 contribution to any one federal candidate in any election cycle (primary, runoff primary, general election), that same person can give more than $30,000 to a national political party and another $10,000 to that party's state and local committees, which can then use this money to increase the party's influence over the candidate and consequently, if he or she wins, over a sitting member of the Senate or House of Representatives. (House Minority Leader Nancy Pelosi, determined to regain her role as Speaker should the Democrats once again find themselves in control of the House, threw herself so vigorously into political fund-raising that, by November 2011, a full year before the next congressional elections, Politico reported, she had boosted the treasury of the Democratic Congressional Campaign Committee by $26 million, a 44 percent increase over the amount she raised during 2007 and 2009.)[2] Nick Nyhart, the president of the nonprofit campaign reform organization Public Campaign, notes that in 1983–84, when Ronald Reagan was president and Tip O'Neill was House Speaker, the Democratic Congressional Campaign Committee—the political arm of House Democrats—raised just $10.4 million; in 2010, the committee raised nearly $164 million.[3] The parties even try to influence the flow of money to opposition candidates: in April 2010, according to the Capitol Hill newspaper *Roll Call*, Republican Congressman Greg Walden, deputy chair of the party's congressional (campaign) committee, "called out more than 100 downtown political action committee representatives . . . for giving too much cash to Democrats."[4] According to the article, Walden allegedly "showcased an internal analysis" of the corporate political action committees that were contributing insufficiently to the Republican Party and its candidates.

Political parties raise money at the state and local level too; a national political party plus its Senate campaign committee and its state and local affiliates may together toss nearly $50,000 into a candidate's war chest. In close races and in states with relatively small populations, that infusion of funds for television advertising, phone banks, and get-out-the-vote efforts may be decisive. The winning candidate is then likely to go to Washington committed to sticking with his or her party (this is certainly the aim of Pelosi's prodigious fund-raising efforts), thus further widening the partisan divide and making independent thought and political compromise much more difficult and perhaps impossible.

Political parties can play even more decisive roles in state legislative races, and they often do so, not only to affect the drafting of state law but, when it comes time to redraw district lines for the legislature and for congressional seats, to bind legislators more closely to party leaders. A prime example was the 2011 elections for seats in the Virginia House of Delegates, in which Democrats held a narrow 22–18 majority. Because the state's lieutenant governor presides over the Senate, a Republican gain of just two seats would have created a tie that could then be broken in the Republicans' favor by the vote of Republican Lieutenant Governor Bill Bolling. This was therefore a crucial election, with the underlying premise on both sides being that the newly elected legislators would vote the party line. By September 30, more than a month before the election, Democratic incumbent William Roscoe Reynolds had received $70,000 from his party, while the Republican Party had given nearly four times as much—$265,000—to his challenger, William Stanley, Jr. Senate candidates also benefited from an infusion of party funds: John S. Edwards (Democrat), $55,000, and David Nutter (Republican), more than $100,000; Edward Houck (Democratic incumbent), $65,500, and Bryce Reeves (Republican), $55,500; John Miller (Democratic incumbent), $50,000, and Mickey Chohany (Republican), $53,150.

Ranging from $50,000 up to as much as a quarter of a million dollars, these figures are especially significant because these were not congressional elections, in which districts averaged nearly 700,000 people, but seats in a state legislature, for which district populations averaged just over 175,000. Nationally, according to Public Campaign's Nyhart, the Republican State Leadership Committee and Democratic Legislative Campaign Committee together spent nearly $41 million on state legislative elections in 2010, $33 million more than they had spent just six years earlier. There is simply no other justification for such a massive outlay of cash for a single state legislative seat beyond the clear knowledge by party leaders that the people they help elect not only will do their bidding on decisions that shape state laws, but will also influence the balance of power in the U.S. House of Representatives—and thus spell victory or defeat for major pieces of national legislation.

But parties need not rely on direct contributions from their own treasuries to shape public policy; super-PACs have created new avenues for party domination. On October 30, 2011, the *New York Times* carried a front-page story with the headline "Outside Groups Eclipsing G.O.P. as Hub of Campaigns Next Year."[5] But the headline was misleading: the super-PACs the article referred to, like American Crossroads, the American Action Network, and Americans for Prosperity, do not supplant the party's fund-raising and campaign-spending apparatus, as the article suggests, but are new tools for the party to use, advancing Republican positions unimpeded by restrictions that would apply to the party itself. American Crossroads and another super-PAC, Crossroads GPS, are run by Karl Rove, who had been President George W. Bush's chief political adviser; Steven Law, the former executive director of the National Republican Senatorial Committee; and Mike Duncan, a former Republican national chair. American Crossroads' political director, Carl Forti, is the former communications director of the National Republican Congressional Committee (NRCC); the communications director, Jonathan Collegio, was the NRCC's press secretary; one of the principal fund-raisers, Haley Barbour, is another former national chair of the Republican Party (and former governor of Mississippi); John Boehner, the Speaker of the House and the highest-ranking Republican official in the nation, also raises money for the organization, according to the *Times*. As Yale law professor Heather Gerken puts it, "Karl Rove was once inside the White House; now he is running a shadow Republican Party that has no formal authority but hundreds of millions of dollars in its war chest." Writing on the website Politico in October 2011, reporters Anna Palmer and Jim VandeHei noted that "in the past few weeks, Speaker John Boehner and House Majority Leader Eric Cantor have endorsed new super PACs while House Minority Leader Nancy Pelosi and Senate Majority Leader Harry Reid have been aggressively fundraising for their favored Super PACs—likely the start of a practice about to explode."[6]

Ed Gillespie, yet another former national party chair, runs another super-PAC, the Republican State Leadership Committee; Brian Walsh, the NRCC's former political director, is president of the super-PAC American Action Network; Tom Reynolds, a former NRCC chair, is on the board of the Congressional Leadership Fund super-PAC. Make Us Great Again is a super-PAC that said it hoped to raise $55 million on behalf of Texas Governor Rick Perry; it's run by Mike Toomey, Perry's former chief of staff. According to the *Washington Post*, the super-PAC Restore Our Future PAC, which supports Mitt Romney, "was co-founded by several former Romney aides."[7] Law, the president of American Crossroads, told the *New York Times* that Republican donors supported his group because they believe "we have the party's best interests at heart—that there is a strong identification with a Republican platform and Republican leadership."[8]

The *Times* reported that Crossroads hoped to raise and spend

$240 million during the 2012 elections and that other organizations planned to spend as much as $200 million. The connection between these "independent" fund-raising organizations and the political parties becomes even more obvious when we look at the role the party plays in facilitating the gathering of massive amounts of money. The *Times* reports that the Republican National Committee (RNC) had contracted with a company called Data Trust to manage the party's huge database of contributors, the RNC's most important asset, and "to swap the list with other outside groups, which can use money raised outside federal contribution limits to update it." The *Times* then added that "under current law, the improved list can then be used by the Republican National Committee, potentially saving the party millions of dollars." It should not come as a surprise that Data Trust is run by the RNC's former chief of staff.

While these examples focus on the aggressive fund-raising tactics of the Republican Party—a tool that will make Republican candidates even more dependent on remaining in the good graces of party leaders—the Democrats are doing the same thing. The second-largest super-PAC after American Crossroads is one organized to support President Obama, founded and led by Democratic Party insiders. The pro-Obama super-PAC, Priorities USA Action, the *Washington Post* reported, is run by Bill Burton, a former spokesman for the Obama White House.[9]

Oklahoma Congressman Tom Cole, a former chair of the National Republican Congressional Committee (the campaign arm of the House Republican Conference), told Politico that while there are limits to how much lawmakers can coordinate with super-PACs, the distance between outside groups and candidates is mostly on paper. "When your old consultants and your best buddies are setting them up, you can pretty much suspect there's been a lot of discussion beforehand."[10] Because they will be able to influence who actually gets elected, Cole warned, super-PACs will be "much worse than lobbying, much more dangerous."

Members of Congress have also begun to create their own campaign funding structures to help elect other candidates of the same political party. Supporters who have contributed the legal maximum ($2,500 per election cycle) to a congressperson's reelection campaign may then give an additional $5,000 to a "leadership" political action committee that the congressperson can use to support other candidates, thereby creating in the recipient not only an obligation to the political party but an indebtedness to specific party leaders, who can call in those "chits" not only to win votes for specific legislation but also to gain support for their campaigns within the party caucus to win powerful leadership positions. When Representative Tom DeLay of Texas was elected Republican whip (then the party's third-highest leadership position in the House of Representatives), it was his leadership PAC's contributions to first-term House members that enabled him to defeat more senior House members, including Pennsylvania Congressman Bob Walker, who had been the party's chief deputy whip.

There are many concerns about the current campaign financing system and many suggestions for changing it. Most of them have problems. One frequently heard proposal is to take private money out of the picture altogether by creating a system of public financing similar to that available to presidential candidates who agree to limit their overall campaign expenditures. (Notably, however, both of the most recent successful presidential candidates, George W. Bush and Barack Obama, chose not to participate in the public financing system. The Internal Revenue Service reports that the proportion of taxpayers who have chosen to contribute to the system dropped from nearly 20 percent in 1990 to less than 7 percent in 2010, leading to several congressional attempts to end the system altogether.) Arizona, Maine, and Connecticut have adopted public financing systems for their state elections, but there are at least two strong arguments against public financing of congressional elections. It is certain, for example, that your taxes would help elect to powerful public positions some men and women with whom you have profound disagreements. When David Duke, the former Ku Klux Klan leader, ran for Congress in Louisiana, he might well have received tax dollars from people who found his views repugnant if there had been a public financing system. On the other hand, if the pool of government funds available for congressional candidates were filled only by voluntary contributions, as with the presidential funding system, it is highly unlikely that there would be enough money in the system to allow candidates to conduct competitive campaigns. In 2007, Common Cause, a nonprofit lobby and advocacy group that supports public financing, reported that voluntary contributions were insufficient to keep up with the cost of presidential campaigns and that the system could become insolvent if most candidates were to accept public funds.[11] And that's just for presidential campaigns, not for the 435 U.S. House races and 33 or 34 Senate races every general-election cycle. If public funds were available in primaries as well, thousands of candidates either would have their ambitions paid for by the taxpayers or would share tiny slivers of a small pool of money drawn from voluntary contributions.

That is a pragmatic argument, but there are other reasons to think that public financing is not the answer to political campaign funding. Democracy is not a spectator sport: it requires a participating citizenry. Today, hundreds of thousands of men and women who neither run for public office nor have the time to work actively in campaigns nonetheless help shape public policy by sending contributions, often in quite small amounts, to the candidates who best reflect their views and best understand their concerns. A vibrant democracy demands more, not less, participation; more, not fewer, citizens willing to help determine who will make the nation's laws. Increasingly, the United States fights wars in which soldiers die but nonsoldiers go about their daily lives unaffected; America as a national enterprise and Americans as the presumed directors of that enterprise are increasingly disconnected. If government supplants the role of the citizen in the election process, democracy will be weakened still further.

Another popular approach to campaign finance reform is to focus not on the source of campaign funds but on the amounts spent. The most common proposals involve either limiting the duration of campaigns (assuming one would spend less in a ninety-day Senate campaign than in one lasting six to nine months) or setting a limit on how much a candidate could spend on his or her election, regardless of how long that campaign lasted. Both methods present the same dilemma: shortening campaigns or reducing the ability of candidates to buy advertising would inevitably provide voters with less information. As the weeks go by, opponents and journalists learn more about a candidate's personal and political history in ways that can affect their decisions. At the presidential level, for example, news of George W. Bush's arrest for driving under the influence of alcohol came to public attention only a few days before the 2000 election. And presidential candidates campaign under intense and unremitting scrutiny; it is even harder for voters to sufficiently inform themselves about candidates for Congress, especially in the many congressional districts that no longer contain major newspapers or television outlets with staffs of investigative reporters. Voters' opinions may not change as more information becomes available, but more information is far better than not enough.

Limiting campaign spending has a similar effect. In addition, given the high cost of campaigning, every limitation on what a candidate can do to reach voters will necessarily increase that candidate's dependence on support from his or her political party. When the candidate is elected and becomes a member of Congress, he or she will know very well the risks of alienating party support and will be highly vulnerable to party leaders' insistence on issue solidarity, on resistance to compromise, on being a loyal foot soldier in a never-ending war for partisan advantage in which serving the national interest may take second place in a legislator's priorities.

So, what to do?

First, allow campaign contributions only from a candidate's prospective constituents. The argument can be made that all citizens should be allowed to contribute to a congressional campaign because members of Congress write laws for the entire nation (when the Congress approves tax increases, all the nation's citizens who fit within the designated categories are subject to the rates the Congress has established; when the Congress approves going to war, all of America goes to war). We all have a stake in what each member of Congress does. But while the Constitution spells out a collective grant of national authority for the legislative branch, it also clearly delineates whose representative or senator each member of Congress is. It is not unreasonable to suggest, as Tennessee Congressman Jim Cooper has done, that just as no one other than a candidate's prospective constituents may vote in that particular election, only those same constituents should be authorized to cast a figurative "vote" with their dollars.

More than a quarter-century ago, the House Republican Policy Committee, which I then chaired, wrestled with the question of limiting sources of campaign funding. It was not an entirely altruistic undertaking: Republicans were concerned that wealthy liberals in Manhattan and Hollywood were funneling huge infusions of cash into distant congressional campaigns, overwhelming the efforts of local citizens. The resulting proposals focused on requiring that either all or most of a candidate's contributions come from within the contested constituency. Focusing on the position that a member of

Congress was to be "representative" of a community, some argued for expanding the circle of permissible contributions to include not only citizens of a specific congressional district, but also those of adjoining districts, on the theory that the successful candidate would be representing the larger community as well. While I represented Oklahoma City and several of its suburbs, for example, residents of adjoining suburbs would also benefit—or suffer—as a result of my efforts. They therefore had a stake in the elections in which I was a candidate. Others argued, on the same basis, that all residents of a state should be permitted to contribute to the congressional campaigns of any federal candidate in that state. The one thing all proposals had in common was that only those with a direct stake in a specific congressperson's performance should be involved in determining the outcome of that race. At the time, Democrats were as adamantly opposed to such reforms as Republicans were enthusiastic about them. The reason was simple: many constituencies in which liberals had a good chance for victory consisted of large numbers of people with limited financial resources; to buy enough advertising to compete, Democrats argued, they needed cash from outside their districts. It was not an unfair argument, but today's world is quite different. Money still pours into the campaigns of liberal candidates from those same wealthy communities in New York and Hollywood, but now it flows into conservative campaigns as well from well-organized and equally wealthy Republican funders.

One can obviously make a legitimate argument that because the votes cast by every member of Congress affect the fortunes of all Americans equally, a Republican in Idaho should be permitted to support an effort to defeat a Democrat in Indiana, and a Democrat in New York should be able to help a Democrat in Nevada win an election against a Republican opponent. We are, after all, one nation, and I cannot completely discount such a position. Nor can I claim that limiting contributions as Cooper has suggested would pass constitutional muster, given the Supreme Court's broad support of political spending as a protected form of speech. But so long as candidates' campaigns are funded by like-minded partisans with no connection to the constituency the candidates are to represent, it is one's party, not one's constituents, that will wield the strongest influence on the winning candidate's subsequent actions. If we are to make members of Congress less dependent on partisans who demand unflagging loyalty to "the team," one way to start is to return control of campaigns to the voters whose preferences and interests should, in a workable democracy, trump any loyalty to outside interests, including one's political party.

Second, make political campaigns less expensive. Many observers have argued that campaigns are so costly, and the need to raise campaign funds so oppressive, that members of Congress are increasingly drawn away from their legislative responsibilities to spend their time attending fund-raising events or making phone calls to prospective contributors. While most candidates leave most of the time-consuming work of identifying potential contributors, arranging events, and even soliciting donations to finance committees, the sheer weight of dollars needed inevitably demands the candidate's personal participation. Michael Malbin, the executive director of the Washington-based Campaign Finance Institute, regularly compiles campaign spending data for the institute's book *Vital Statistics on Congress*. In 2008, Malbin found, a campaign for a seat in the U.S. House of Representatives typically cost nearly $1.4 million.[12] With two years between one election and the next, House members would have to raise an average of more than $10,000 a week to come up with the needed funds. Because senatorial campaigns are run statewide, most Senate races are considerably more expensive. For example, in the 2000 elections, Jon Corzine, running in New Jersey, spent more than $63 million, and Hillary Clinton in New York nearly $30 million. But whether it's Corzine's $63 million or a House race costing $1.4 million, the money needed to get into Congress is mind-numbing. Instead of simply accepting the high cost as inevitable and trying to find ways to provide the funds, we should reverse the process and make campaigns less costly. This would reduce candidate dependence on both special interests and party leaders who demand that elected officials march in lockstep on important issues. Here are some ways that can be accomplished.

In 1934, the Congress declared the broadcast frequencies used by radio and television stations to be "public" airwaves. The Federal Communications Commission describes the attendant responsibilities this way: "In exchange for obtaining a valuable license to operate a broadcast station using the public airwaves, each radio and television licensee is required by law to operate its station in the 'public interest, convenience and necessity.' This means that it must air programming that is responsive to the needs and problems of its local community of license. . . . Station licensees, as the trustees of the public's airwaves, must use the broadcast medium to serve the public interest."[13]

The truth is, no candidate likes to raise money; it is demeaning to ask friends to contribute to help one get elected; it is like walking a tightrope to seek, and accept, campaign contributions with an awareness that at some point the contributor may show up in your Washington office expecting your help in passing or defeating a legislative proposal. Moreover, the time it takes to raise large sums of money reduces time available to study issues, advance one's own political interests, or spend time with one's family. Candidates nonetheless devote large portions of their lives, both before and after the election, to seeking ever more funds for the campaign treasury. No campaign can succeed without the means to convey the candidate's character, experience, and policies to the electorate. Even in the twenty-first century, with its emphasis on websites, Facebook, Twitter, and other new media, radio and especially television are indispensable to a political campaign. Rather than willingly help in the process of informing voters, broadcasters charge excessively high rates both for air time and for the production of campaign commercials. In almost every race for a seat in Congress, whether for the House or Senate, television advertising constitutes a giant chunk of the campaign budget.

An important step, then, is to require radio and television stations—using the public airwaves—to provide a limited amount of free air time to every qualified candidate for federal office. By itself, this will not provide equal reach into citizens' homes—it will not provide free newspaper advertising or air time on cable television stations, nor can stations be reasonably expected to provide a steady flow of such advertising—but it will narrow the advantage that richer candidates have and ensure that all have an opportunity to put their candidacies before the people. Each state makes its own election laws, including laws governing the election of federal officials, and states differ in defining legitimate candidacies. Most require either a specified filing fee or a predetermined number of signatures of registered voters—necessary "weeding out" systems to prevent clogging the ballot with marginal candidates with little support. But for those who qualify—and this number will be more than the two candidates the major parties now allow us to choose between—the chance of being heard will be significantly increased.

That, of course, is not enough. Incumbents in Congress are able to send "franked" mail to their constituents—mail that requires only the legislator's signature on an envelope (the signature may be stamped or, more commonly, preprinted). Even though there is a limit to the number of frankable letters and newsletters that can be sent to constituents in a year, with cutoff dates in advance of elections, the franking privilege is a clear advantage. Assuming, however, that states have implemented criteria to ensure that only serious candidates qualify, they, too, can be permitted to send a free letter to each registered voter within the constituency. One free mailing to every household will not offset the more frequent mailings from incumbents or the paid mailings from better-funded campaigns, but along with the free radio and television time, it will help close the gap.

Even those changes can be supplemented. In some states (California, for example), voters receive, before each election, a mailing that lists the various referenda and initiatives to be voted on, with statements by supporters and opponents outlining their arguments. The same mailings can easily be expanded to include statements of background and policy positions by qualified candidates for federal office. Some candidates will always have more to spend and will appear more frequently on constituents' television screens or in their mailboxes, but no legitimate candidate will be denied the opportunity to get his or her message in front of every voter. This would reduce the dominance of party-endorsed candidates and provide a somewhat more level playing field, simultaneously reducing the need for massive expenditures and increasing voter choice.

Ironically—and counterintuitively—Curtis Gans of American University, one of the nation's leading election scholars and a strong critic of the shrill partisanship in contemporary American politics, has proposed not reducing campaign spending but doing the opposite: removing the existing limits—but with the requirement that the contributions be made directly to the candidates, the only persons in the process who could be held accountable by voters. Gans blames much of the current low tone in political contests on the influence of win-at-all-costs campaign consultants and the anything-goes advertising messages they construct, and he has advocated legislation that would mandate that television advertising promoting a candidacy feature either the purchaser of the ad or an identified spokesperson speaking the message directly into the television camera— in other words, sunshine as a disinfectant.

Political campaigns are essential to any modern democratic system of government. The days when one could run for president without leaving one's front porch are behind us: today, candidates for public office need an opportunity to describe their qualifications and policy proposals, and voters need to be able to see, hear, and evaluate them. But public office should not go to the highest bidder. In a system in which money determines who will make our laws, in which private interests—including the private power-seeking clubs known as "parties"—can dominate the electoral conversation by spending massive amounts of unregulated money, with no transparency as to whose money it is, democracy itself is destroyed. Many years ago, when I was the campaign manager for a candidate for Congress, I received a late-night phone call from a man I knew, an executive with a large corporation, asking me to meet him in the middle of the night in a wheat field in central Oklahoma. There he handed me a briefcase stuffed with cash—a contribution to my candidate's campaign. It was perfectly legal: under the campaign laws of that time, huge amounts of cash could be given anonymously, secretly, in the middle of a wheat field in the dead of night. The secrecy was only a precaution lest the other candidate—the incumbent— learn of the contribution and perhaps retaliate if he were reelected.

Times changed: by the time I ran for office a dozen years later, a corporation could not contribute a postage stamp or a chair to sit in; unreported cash contributions could not exceed $100; total contributions from an individual could not exceed $1,000; contributions from a political action committee could not exceed $5,000; contributions had to be reported, promptly and frequently, and contributors had to be listed by name, address, occupation, and employer. Democracy was flourishing. Special interests could lobby, could get their members or employees to write and call, but they could not dictate; no corporation, labor union, or political party could demand subservience to its interests. Money in politics strengthens the grip of each, putting candidates—and the elected officials they become—at the mercy of those interests who can anoint them with dollars or withhold their favors in the absence of sufficient loyalty. It is a dangerous trend, and our democracy will not survive unless it is reversed. If we cannot control who provides the money, we must make the money less necessary—or surrender the conceit that our political system can be honestly called self-government.

PART III

Reforming the Governing System

SIX

Government Leaders, Not Party Leaders

I always voted at my party's call and I never thought of thinking for
myself at all.
—Sir Joseph in Gilbert and Sullivan's *HMS Pinafore*,
explaining how he rose from a seat in Parliament to become
Lord Admiral of the British Navy

Step Four: Establish a Nonpartisan Congressional Leadership

When Nancy Pelosi became Speaker of the House of Representatives
in 2007 she told an interviewer that one of her goals as Speaker—
the head of the legislative branch of government, ranking behind
only the vice president in the line of succession to the presidency—
was to elect more members of her own party. Regardless of the im-
mense responsibilities inherent in chairing what may be the most
powerful lawmaking body in world history, one of Pelosi's first in-
stincts in those years before Barack Obama's election to the presidency was to see herself not just as the head of America's national
legislature but as the leader of her party.

She had many examples to show the way. Her predecessor, Dennis Hastert, a Republican, often acted as though he thought his job
was to serve as de facto floor leader for the Republican president,
thereby diminishing the role of the House of Representatives as an

independent and coequal part of American government. He apparently defined his responsibilities largely in terms of party label.

Consider how the attitudes of Dennis Hastert, Nancy Pelosi, and others who put party solidarity near the top of their list of priorities have dealt a damaging blow to the separation of powers at the heart of the American constitutional system. As the nation has grown and issues have become increasingly complex, and as the rise of broadcast media has tended to focus national attention more narrowly on the presidency, Congress has increasingly failed to grasp that it is a separate and independent branch of government with a constitutional obligation to serve as a check on the executive. Instead, members of the president's party have tended to see him as their "leader," and members of the other party have seen him as the opposition, to be stymied whenever possible. During the presidencies of Ronald Reagan and George H. W. Bush, with Democrats in control of Congress, Republicans aggressively pushed for a proposal to give presidents, rather than Congress, the final word on federal spending decisions, even though that authority had been deliberately placed in the legislative branch to ensure that the people, through their representatives, would set national priorities. Their loyalty firmly rooted in party identity, Republicans also promised to limit the terms (and influence) of legislators; the goal was to force incumbent Democrats out of office and help Republicans gain a majority, but the effect would have been to strengthen the presidency and undermine a fundamental tenet of American government. That both schemes were clearly unconstitutional, and later found to be so even by a Republican-dominated Supreme Court, was no deterrent to the aggressive pursuit of party advantage.

This circular formulation—the president is the nation's leader, the president is a member of our party, the president is therefore the leader of our party, it is therefore our job to serve our leader—is profoundly and dangerously antidemocratic and can lead to disturbing consequences. Under Hastert's speakership, Republican members of Congress never protested the Republican president's insistence on his right to decide for himself whether he was bound by federal law; they acquiesced to increased executive secrecy and to presidential assertions that the Congress could not require federal departments and agencies to comply with laws the Congress had enacted. When Harry Truman was a senator from Missouri, a Democrat in a legislature controlled by his own party, with a fellow Democrat in the White House, he nonetheless undertook a far-reaching and ultimately highly critical investigation of the War Department and its cozy relationships with profiteering suppliers. Today it's hard to imagine a serious investigation of a Democratic administration by congressional Democrats or of a Republican administration by Republicans.

Before Pelosi, before Hastert, there was Newt Gingrich, another Republican Speaker, and the person who most clearly exemplifies the ways in which party identity and the partisan pursuit of power have eroded the ability of the United States Congress to fulfill its constitutional obligations. As Speaker of the House—occupying one of the country's most important constitutional offices—Gingrich spent hours while on the public payroll plotting how to elect more members of his own party. Instead of merely raising money for their own reelection campaigns, Republican members of Congress were pressured to raise large amounts of additional money to defeat Democrats. Whether the targeted Democrats were liberal or conservative, whether they crossed party lines to support Republican positions, was irrelevant: all that mattered was the party label they wore. Party loyalty became the key to advancement within the House, and it was measured by how much money one could raise. To meet these demands, and to increase their chances of gaining a committee chairmanship or a leadership position within the party, members began to exert fund-raising pressure of their own, leaning hard on those members of the business and professional communities whose profitability could be seriously affected by the passage or the nonpassage of specific legislation. Regulators are usually concerned with lobbyists showering money on legislators, but now the situation was reversed: legislators were extracting money from lobbyists in order to meet their assigned fund-raising goals. Failure to do so could mean being denied an important committee or subcommittee chairmanship because Gingrich, exercising dictatorial authority, handpicked chairmen from among those who had proven they would remain faithful to the "team" and its partisan agenda.

While Gingrich was exceptional in the audacity of his quest to concentrate power in his own hands, other Speakers have also attempted to dictate the work of the House. In September 2010, former House Parliamentarian Charles Johnson, speaking at the Woodrow Wilson Center for International Scholars, decried the corrosive partisanship in Congress and tied the problem directly to Pelosi. Johnson and William McKay, former Clerk of the British House of Commons, in their book *Parliament and Congress*, wrote that Pelosi, through her authority as Speaker and her ability to control the Rules Committee, was able to "dictate a process . . . to supersede committee work products" and "minimize" the ability of Republican members of Congress to offer amendments or participate in House-Senate conferences to reconcile differences between bills passed by the two houses.[1] Don Wolfensberger, director of the Wilson Center's Congress Project and former staff director of the House Rules Committee, wrote in *Roll Call* that he hoped party leaders could still lead "by setting a tone and operating style that encourage and reward Member participation in the legislative process."[2]

The Senate has grown partisan more slowly, largely because its rules place more power in the hands of individual senators, but it is hardly immune from the partisan warfare that has enveloped the

House. While Harry Reid, the Majority Leader, is known for his dismissive attitude toward Senate Republicans, it is his Republican counterpart, Mitch McConnell, who has played the Pelosi role in the Senate. Soon after Barack Obama's election, McConnell told a reporter that his goal was to make Obama a one-term president. Conservative talk-show host Rush Limbaugh had stirred controversy by saying, just days after Obama's inauguration, that he hoped the president would fail, but Limbaugh has no official responsibilities; he is merely a paid talker, raking in a sizable personal fortune by being quotable and rousing passions. (Once, when I was a guest on the radio program of his fellow talk-show host Laura Ingraham, she responded to my criticisms of Limbaugh by arguing—during a commercial break—that I should not have criticized Limbaugh for his remarks because "it's just entertainment.") McConnell, on the other hand, is Minority Leader of the United States Senate. He has responsibilities Limbaugh and Ingraham do not have: his job is not "entertainment"—but in this instance his instinct was to position himself not as a leading legislator but as spokesman for a political club.

When New York Congressman Charles Rangel, then the chair of the House Ways and Means Committee (which writes the nation's tax laws) announced that he was stepping down temporarily from his chairmanship in the midst of an ethics investigation, he declared that he was doing it for the good of . . . his party, which he feared might be hurt by the negative attention he was receiving. When Obama's health care bill was advancing through the House of Representatives, Byron York, chief political correspondent for the *Washington Examiner*, wrote of Democrats who were wavering in their support for the bill, "If you think House Speaker Nancy Pelosi is going to let them off easy . . . well, that's not gonna happen. . . . In the hallways and the hideaways of Capitol Hill, the Democratic message is clear: Real men don't cross the party. Understand?"[3]

Both the "team" concept and partisan warfare have become central parts of the legislative world. Both parties maintain active campaign organizations within both the House and Senate, and the leaders of those organizations hold official party leadership positions. Chairing your party's campaign committee, raising substantial amounts of money to defeat members of the other party, presiding over an election in which your party gains more seats or loses fewer than anticipated, can become a major advantage in positioning yourself to move up the ranks—not just in your party, but in the House or Senate. An article in *Setting Course*, a publication of the nonpartisan Congressional Management Foundation, described the current "culture of Congress" this way: "In the past several years, the rhetoric has grown hot. . . . Tensions have run high as leaders lob charges of obstructionism at each other. . . . In the House, vigorous debate has occasionally escalated into instances of name-calling, and in one or two high profile cases, near fistfights."[4] The article went on to quote a June 2000 article in the *Washington Post:* "The fundamental problems that caused a virtual shutdown of Senate business before the Memorial Day recess—including policy disputes, personal tensions, power struggles and the pressure-cooker atmosphere of an election year—remain as threatening as ever. They lurk just beneath the surface, ready to explode again when a new provocation occurs."

The *National Journal* summarized the problem in a lengthy article at the end of February 2011, just as the new Congress shaped by the "Tea Party" election of 2010 was beginning its work:

> At the broadest level, the trends in NJ's [*National Journal's*] vote ratings over the past three decades track the decline of individualism in Congress. Throughout congressional history, the most respected legislators—from Henry Clay and Stephen Douglas to Lyndon Johnson, Bob Dole, and Edward Kennedy—have been those who through force of personality or intellect have

been able to assemble coalitions and forge compromises that would not have coalesced without them. Such personalized acts of consensus-building still occur but much less frequently, and those who try face much steeper walls of resistance to compromise. . . . Primarily, legislators in both chambers (especially the House) are asked to simply be foot soldiers—to support policy choices that their leadership forges, almost always in close consultation with the constituency groups central to the party's coalition. Rather than being heralded as iconoclasts, those legislators who deviate too often from that centrally directed consensus now face pressure from their colleagues; a cold shoulder from leadership; blistering criticism from the overtly partisan media aligned with each side; and with growing frequency, primary challenges bankrolled by powerful party interest groups.[5]

As former Senator Lowell Weicker told *National Journal* reporter Ronald Brownstein, "The overarching point is that the Senate was comprised of 100 individuals who had a loose binding with the respective parties. . . . You had people who stood on their own two feet." Weicker, then a Republican, served three terms in the Senate before he was defeated by Joseph Lieberman in 1988; two years later he was elected governor of Connecticut as an Independent.

But it is futile to demand less partisanship from an institution that is based on partisanship. In the House of Representatives, the division into warring camps begins in the very first hour of a member's service. I was elected to the House as a partisan—I ran as a Republican and won the general election by defeating a Democrat—but, raising my hand to take the oath of office the following January, standing in a chamber ringed by the images of history's great lawmakers, I felt as though I had stepped across an important line; I was no longer a Republican candidate but a member of the lawmaking body of the most powerful nation on Earth. With that oath I assumed a great responsibility. The other brand-new members of Congress alongside me did the same—Al Gore and Dick Gephardt, both of whom later ran for president; Dan Quayle, who, like Gore, served as vice president; David Stockman, who became Ronald Reagan's budget director; Jim Leach, who served in the House longer than any of us before becoming the director of the National Endowment for the Humanities—all of us starting on a new path in American government. At that moment, in that chamber, with parents and spouses watching from the balconies and small children in the arms of the members as they stood on the House floor, we were all one, and America's future rested in large part on our shoulders. At that moment, we were not "teams," and if a child had broken loose from its father's or mother's arms and scurried through the hall, none of us would have known, or cared, if the child's parents were Republicans or Democrats. Then the moment passed.

As soon as we took our oaths of office, we elected a new Speaker. The Democrats had met earlier in caucus and nominated Tip O'Neill for Speaker. We Republicans (who call our organization a "conference" rather than a "caucus") had nominated Congressman John Rhodes of Arizona. Democrats voted for the Democrat, Republicans voted for the Republican. Soon we adopted House rules (written by the majority party) and established party ratios on House committees. The majority party had determined the ratios and had a comfortable margin on each committee—far more than comfortable on some, such as the Rules Committee, which determines whether a bill or amendment can be considered. The process continues to this day—harmony for an instant, division from then on. The pattern is set on the first day: votes were cast not based on the individual member's judgment as to whether O'Neill or Rhodes would be the better manager of the House, or whether the committees would function more fairly if party representation were equal, or whether it would be better if all amendments with a legitimate base of support were permitted to come to the floor; votes were cast as a bloc, according to one's team membership. That is how the Congress operates. Thought is replaced by reflex: men and women who offered themselves to voters as "leaders" become members of a herd, not leading but following. Members of Congress who moments before had taken an oath of loyalty to the Constitution were exhibiting a new loyalty—to a political club.

There have been attempts to paint today's hyperpartisanship and the resulting legislative dysfunction as merely the marks of a particular historical period that dates from the Gingrich speakership. But the problem is of long standing. Gingrich can fairly be blamed for the fuel he recklessly splashed about, but the partisan flames were already eating away at Congress before he rose to power. Kathryn Pearson, a political scientist at the University of Minnesota, wrote in the *Boston Review* that "party leaders acquired their most significant tools under the Democratic reforms of the 1970s, when Democrats took power away from committees and empowered party leaders and the Democratic Caucus . . . giving the speaker much more control over the legislative agenda and members' careers."[6] In 1975, "Democrats ousted three committee chairs, and party loyalty increased among those who kept their posts. Democrats empowered the leadership-controlled Steering and Policy Committee to make committee assignments. The speaker was authorized to select the chair and Democratic members of the House Rules Committee, rendering the Committee a tool of the leadership." When Representative Jim Wright of Texas succeeded Tip O'Neill as Speaker, Pearson writes, he "articulated a partisan legislative agenda, expanded leaders' powers, and used procedural maneuvers to block Republican-supported amendments." Nor was this just a matter of Wright's personal leadership style; partisan policy battles continued under Wright's successor, Democrat Tom Foley.

After Foley, Democrats lost control of the House for a decade, but when they regained the majority, the partisanship escalated. "Even with an influx of Democrats from swing districts in 2006 and 2008, Democrats were more unified under [Nancy] Pelosi's leadership than ever before," Pearson wrote, "not only voting together at record levels, but raising more money for the party and for one another, too."

It's time to change the system at the very top, in the operation of the Congress itself.

The United States Constitution states that the members of the House of Representatives shall choose their own Speaker (in other words, their "spokesman" and leader). In the Senate, the Majority Leader exercises similar powers even though the vice president is technically the "president" of the Senate. There are no rules, except those the two houses have created, that determine who is eligible to lead those bodies or how one is to be chosen for the position. Therefore we have a free hand to decide how things should be done to give the American people a legislative branch that is driven by the public good, not the interests of a political party.

Let's begin with the office of Speaker. Here there are three separate questions: Who may serve as Speaker? How is the Speaker to be elected? What role should the Speaker serve? The answer to the first question seems obvious enough: whichever member of Congress gets the greatest number of votes from his or her House colleagues. But the truth is less obvious. There is no requirement in the Constitution that the Speaker be a member of Congress. It is quite possible for a House member to nominate for the speakership a respected American who does not serve in Congress. It could be a former government official like Colin Powell, a former secretary of state and chair of the Joint Chiefs of Staff; or David Boren, a former senator and now a university president; or Norman Mineta, a former member of Congress who has served in the cabinets of both

Republican and Democratic presidents; or it could be a mayor like Michael Bloomberg, an Independent; or a prominent business leader. The only criteria should be a capacity for competent management, a reputation for integrity, and a commitment to bipartisanship.

Just as the Constitution does not say who can be Speaker, it does not define the Speaker's role. As members of Congress become increasingly locked into their party commitments, and Speakers—always chosen on party-line votes—are viewed not as the chairs of the House but as party leaders, the centralization of authority in the Speaker's hands merely reinforces political group-think. This trend took a particularly troublesome turn when Gingrich became Speaker. Gingrich pushed for—and won—limits on the number of terms a member could serve as a committee chair, cut back funding for unofficial "commonality" groups in the House, and reduced staffing. Superficially, the Gingrich measures looked like, and were promoted as, congressional "reforms." In actuality they were purges: a carefully structured plan to reduce competition from other potential power centers. As the Speaker became the sole repository of legislative authority, centralized control over the party and the party's centralized control over the House became the new norm. In November 2003, the Congressional Research Service (CRS) sponsored a conference titled "The Changing Nature of the Speakership." The published report of the conference included an article by Walter J. Oleszek, the CRS senior specialist in legislative process, and Richard Sachs, CRS specialist in American national government, looking at "catalysts of institutional and procedural change" regarding the speakership and the operation of the House of Representatives. They zeroed in on Gingrich—who, unsurprisingly, had argued that responsible governing "requires greater assets in the leader's office."[7]

"Not only did Gingrich personally select certain Republicans to chair several standing committees . . . he also required the GOP members of the Appropriations Committee to sign a written pledge that they would heed the Republican leadership's recommendations for spending reductions. Furthermore, he often bypassed committees entirely by establishing leadership task forces to process legislation, dictated orders to committee chairs, and used the Rules Committee to redraft committee-reported legislation. Party power during this period dominated committee power." They might have added that party power (in the form of the Speaker) superseded the obligation both to represent constituent concerns and to independently evaluate the best course for the country. While King Louis XIV may have never actually said "L'état c'est moi" (I am the State), it's a good description of the Gingrich speakership, which established an extreme partisanship that has persisted ever since.

We Americans have long assumed that the Speaker is, in fact, supposed to be the partisan leader of whichever political party controls the House. But the Speaker could play a very different role, overseeing a completely nonpartisan division of committees, guaranteeing a nonpartisan process for considering legislation on the House floor, and serving as a mediator to push the competing parties toward common ground and effective problem-solving. In Great Britain, the Speaker of the House of Commons, who has complete control over the chamber's proceedings, is nonpartisan. If an active member of a political party, he or she quits the party on becoming Speaker. The Speaker of the Canadian House of Commons also serves a nonpartisan function. Because human beings always incline toward allegiances and gravitate toward persons who hold views similar to their own, partisanship will not disappear from Congress, no matter who is Speaker. But the entire political process will change if party leaders no longer control it, pushing forward the legislation they favor and consigning bills or amendments they oppose to the legislative trash can.

Having a vision of how a Speaker might operate in a less partisan way does not guarantee that the person selected will actually meet that obligation. Thus it matters greatly how a Speaker is selected. Today, as when I was first elected to the House, each party selects its own candidate for the office and all members vote, aloud, in the House Chamber, on the public record, for the candidate whose name has been put forth by the club they belong to. While there have been occasional defections—usually by a conservative Democrat who names a member neither party has nominated—the vote is almost always straight down the party line: one knows the result days before the votes are actually cast. The solution is to change the voting system in two ways.

First, while there are benefits to transparency—and final votes on all legislation should always be on the record—there are also benefits to nontransparency. In the current political climate, for example, we would likely get better results—and more of the essential compromise on which a populous democracy depends—if legislators were permitted to negotiate privately without fear of being pummeled for "selling out" if they seek ways to advance their principles and still allow government to function. That same concern—allowing government to function—is a strong argument for electing a Speaker by secret ballot, as is done in the British House of Commons. This would allow every member of the House to vote for that candidate he or she actually believes would best perform the functions of Speaker, without being exposed to retaliation for lack of fealty to one's club.

Second, the actual requirements for election should be designed to make strict partisanship almost impossible. There are at least two ways to accomplish this. In Great Britain, to run for Speaker one must have been nominated by a dozen members of the House, and one-third of the nominators must be members of a different political party. Clearly, no candidate who seemed excessively partisan would easily find enough support outside his or her party to meet that requirement. But because there is always the chance that a candidate might make secret arrangements to win the support of the necessary members of an opposition party (it is widely believed that just such backroom dealing may have determined the outcome of the 1824 presidential election, in which John Quincy Adams defeated Andrew Jackson in a race ultimately decided by the House of Representatives), the grassroots group No Labels has proposed an even stricter requirement: to win election as Speaker under that plan a candidate would have to receive the support of at least 60 percent of the members of the House. Such a barrier would almost certainly require any candidate for Speaker to actively reach across the political aisle with promises of cooperation, fairness, and full consideration of policy alternatives.

When Dennis Hastert succeeded Newt Gingrich as Speaker, he readily admitted that he paid attention only to "the majority of the majority"—in other words, only to his fellow Republicans. In the ensuing years, with Hastert as the Speaker and Nancy Pelosi as the leader of House Democrats, the polarization of the House reached new levels. Congressman Jim Cooper, writing in *Boston Review*, observed that "party unity scores, which measure how much the members of a party vote together, rose above 90 percent . . . leadership told members how to vote on most issues and force-fed talking points so that everyone could stay on message . . . all major floor votes became partisan steamrollers . . . no coherent alternatives were allowed to be considered, only approval of party doctrine . . . a member's only choice was being a teammate or a traitor."[8]

Step Five: Establish Nonpartisan Congressional Committees

By itself, changing the role of the Speaker won't change the underlying dysfunctions in Congress. In today's system, party leaders have complete control over appointments to congressional committees. It is a reality of congressional life that the committee assignments members of Congress receive affect their reelection chances: a senator or House member who can actively defend the economic interests of his or her constituency by serving on a committee that directly reflects these concerns will be seen by those constituents as more valuable. Although members of Congress are part of the national government's legislature, each one is also a representative of the concerns and interests of the citizens he or she was chosen to represent. If a representative from a farming community wins appointment to the Agriculture Committee, it matters to voters.

Today, in both the House and Senate, a member's committee assignment is entirely the prerogative of party leaders. Sometimes, the authority to make such decisions is vested in a leadership committee; at other times, the party leader makes committee assignments unilaterally. In either case, the assignments often come with strings attached. Party leaders expect their appointees to carefully hew to the party line on key issues. When Democrats expanded their control of the House of Representatives in 2008, Speaker Pelosi quickly dismissed the idea of a Congress that worked cooperatively, making it clear that because Democrats had won the election, they would write the bills. She had a world-class role model: when Newt Gingrich was Speaker, California Congressman Carlos Moorhead and Tennessee Congressman Jimmy Quillen were denied key committee chairmanships because neither was considered sufficiently aggressive in doing battle against the Democrats on those committees. After Moorhead's death in November 2011, his *Washington Post* obituary noted that "his collegial approach might have doomed him in Gingrich's eyes."[9]

In theory, the committees exist to deliberate about the best solutions to major national problems; in reality, they exist to advance the partisan agenda of a temporary majority—or, for members of the minority, to block that agenda—and it is thus seen as the responsibility of the party's representatives on that committee to champion the party line. In her book *Party Wars: Polarization and the Politics of National Policy Making*, Barbara Sinclair observed that whereas committees once provided the space where bipartisan compromise could be formulated, committee hearings in both the House and Senate have increasingly become arenas for partisan debate.[10] Conference committees, in which representatives of the House and Senate meet together to resolve differences between the two chambers' versions of legislation that both houses have passed, are increasingly used not to work out differences but to ensure that the party leaders' preferred positions survive the process unchanged.

University of Texas political scientist Sean Theriault outlined the practice—and its impact—in his book *Party Polarization in Congress*.[11] After the 1994 elections, he wrote, House Republicans under new Speaker Gingrich "explicitly used loyalty in lieu of seniority in the naming of committee chairs. This change advantaged the Republican Party leadership in two ways. First, it put a premium on casting party-loyal votes for members who wished to become committee chairs. The threat of denying a chairpersonship became a powerful tool for the leadership in encouraging members to vote the party line. Second, increasingly loyal committee chairs were more certain to enact the party program. With tighter controls over who would wield committee gavels, the Republican leadership did not have to worry about a rogue committee chair who would enact a personal agenda rather than the party's platform." Theriault pointed to the experience of Congresswoman Marge Roukema, a moderate Republican from New Jersey who had been a longtime member of the House Banking Committee and who played "a crucial role" in overhauling the regulations governing the financial services industry. She was in line to chair the committee after the 2000 elections, and, as Theriault notes, she would have been the first woman ever to head a major full committee in the House of Representatives. It didn't happen.

Although Roukema had more seniority on the committee, Richard Baker of Louisiana also wanted the chairmanship. So did Mike Oxley of Ohio. Baker, Theriault writes, "was a much more reliable Republican vote than Roukema and was a prodigious fundraiser for the party." Oxley, "like Baker, voted in line with the party leadership and campaigned vigorously for them." Roukema had twenty years of experience as compared with Oxley's nineteen and Baker's fourteen, but experience wasn't what mattered: she voted with the party nearly three-fourths of the time (a 74 percent party unity score), but Oxley stood with the party 89 percent of the time, and Baker 92 percent. Despite having faced very difficult reelection races (first in a primary challenge from a more conservative Republican, then in the general election as a Republican member of Congress from a heavily Democratic state), and despite having had to raise funds for her own campaigns, Roukema had nonetheless raised an additional $40,000 for the party. But Oxley raised more than ten times as much ($420,000), and Baker, whose path to reelection in conservative Louisiana was much easier, raised $1.6 million. Roukema didn't have a chance. Oxley became chair of the committee (renamed the House Financial Services Committee), and Baker became a subcommittee chair. Telling the Associated Press of her "grave disappointment" at being passed over for the chairmanship she had worked toward for two decades, and citing her failure to raise more money for Republican candidates as a reason for having been passed over, Roukema retired.[12] "I was an independent voter in Congress," she told the *Hill*, "and I voted my conscience and my state. That brought me down in [leadership's] estimation. I was not elected to do what leadership [said]. I was elected to do what my intelligence, my conscience, and my constituents needed. . . . That was my reason for being in Congress."[13] Roukema turned down an offer from the Bush administration to be Treasurer of the United States and returned to New Jersey to serve on the boards of several nonprofit organizations dedicated to children's issues. Oxley and Baker eventually left Congress to become lobbyists.

Lawmaking in the United States begins in congressional committees. Once legislation is introduced, it is assigned to a committee, where it may be taken up for consideration or simply ignored; if it is taken up, the committee may hear from witnesses presenting arguments for and against, or it may hear mainly from advocates of the side the majority party favors. It may advance the legislation toward enactment, by passing it and forwarding it to the entire House or Senate for final action, or set it aside. Each of those decisions rests ultimately with the majority party's representatives on the committee. In Congress, party is everything. Here are three ways to change committee members from representatives of their political parties into Americans deliberating together about the nation's future.

First, change the leadership structure of congressional committees. The current system of appointment to committees has no basis in the Constitution; it rests solely on procedural rules adopted by the House and Senate. With enough pressure from constituents, those rules can be changed. One way to start is to ensure that each committee has a chair from the majority party and a vice chair from the minority. Except on certain nonlegislating committees, no such vice chairmanship exists today; the senior, or "ranking," minority member has no authority beyond what the chair grants. The vice chair need not be authorized to ascend to the chairmanship in the chair's absence, but should have the authority to bring a bill forward and invite expert witnesses to offer testimony. The process might be slower, but consideration of the alternatives would be more thorough.

Whichever party holds the majority will resist these changes, since party leaders view the committees as vehicles for enactment of their preferred agenda. The current committee process is transac-

tional, not deliberative. But using committees to bypass true deliberation undercuts the very purpose of a people's legislature.

Second, change the way committee members are appointed.
When I served on the Republican leadership committee that decided other members' committee assignments, I watched as my fellow party leaders sometimes refused to grant a slot to a member
who was seen as too inclined to exercise independent judgment. But
a member of Congress should base his or her decisions on only
three things: a careful understanding of the concerns and interests
of one's constituents, attention to the mandates and prohibitions
of the Constitution, and an independent evaluation of the merits of
the proposal. If congressional committees, with all their power over
the legislative process, are made up of men and women selected
on the basis of something altogether unrelated—fealty to the advancement of a political club—deliberation becomes a charade;
each committee member's mind is made up before the first witness
speaks, even before the proposal has been formally presented.

This method of assigning members to committees is also artificial. It is a practice adopted by the parties to enable them to keep
fractious members (meaning those who insist on thinking for themselves) in line. In every informal congressional subgroup—the Human
Rights Caucus, the Rust Belt Caucus, the Flat Tax Caucus—leaders
are chosen without regard to party affiliation. Imagine how different the lawmaking process would be if that practice prevailed in
committee assignments. If three seats were open on a committee
and five members sought appointment, those seats could be filled by
lot or by seniority. Committee members would thus not be beholden to party leaders for their selection, and would not be fearful
that crossing party lines would cost them their positions. They
would be free to vote as they saw fit. After all, their constituents
chose them not only for their policies but for their temperaments,

knowledge, experience, and values. Eventually, entire committees would be formed without any party division at all—they would be drawn together only by their common interest in solving the problems in the committee's area.

Third, choose committee staff solely on the basis of professional qualifications. Congressional staff members, who work in a congressperson's office and provide the research that senators and representatives use in their deliberations, are chosen to reflect the preferences of the members they serve. On the other hand, committee staff members, who schedule the hearings, invite witnesses to testify, prepare background materials for committee members, and negotiate with staff members from other committees in the House and Senate and with representatives of the executive branch, are generally selected by the committee chair and the ranking minority member. In effect, they are party appointees. But if the goal is to legislate for the country, committee staff should be selected by a nonpartisan House or Senate administrator and obliged to serve all members equally without regard to party agenda.

Note that none of these reforms would take away the ability of the Congress to organize itself, to place individuals in positions of authority, to manage the flow of legislation, or to maintain its own management structure. There would still be a Speaker of the House, there would still be committee chairs, and committees would still choose which legislation to advance to the floor (save for a change that would allow debate and votes on alternatives that received a substantial amount of support from the members), but these decisions would be made without respect to a partisan agenda. Members of a committee—chosen by lot or seniority or some other means not involving selection by party leaders—would be able to vote on a chair and a vice chair, and they could still be from different parties. But no chair could stack the list of witnesses called to give advice about pending legislation, preclude amendments that had significant support, or prevent those amendments from reaching the House floor for consideration. One need not even deny the majority its leading role in shaping the agenda: electoral victory, whether by margins large or small, does matter, and whichever party has more members in the House or Senate will have an advantage in selecting Speakers, Senate leaders, and committee chairs. But the almost absolute power that now flows from being in the majority would be curtailed. All that would change would be to make all members of Congress fully members of Congress regardless of whether their party was in the majority or minority. They would all wear the same label—American—and the same title—Member of Congress.

The impact of partisan "unity," of sticking with the team, of elevating party interest above constituent interest, was summed up nicely in Pearson's *Boston Review* article: "Parties," she wrote, "have become deeply important to members' careers . . . party leaders use their expanding arsenal of tools to exert discipline in pursuit of policy control and to reward rank-and-file members for their loyalty by preferentially determining whose legislation is considered on the House floor, allocating campaign resources, and making committee appointments. In this process of assessing loyalty and assigning rewards, party leaders may forgo opportunities to help their most electorally vulnerable members, those who represent districts where the party's policies are least popular and therefore are most difficult for those members to support. Thus, a member's ability to represent her constituents is affected by leadership goals."[14]

"Narrow margins and fierce partisan competition are likely to persist well into the future," she writes, "suggesting that leaders of both parties will continue to reward loyalty in both voting and fundraising. Partisan polarization in the House will continue unless more members who value their constituents and the reputation of Congress above the reputation of their party stand up to protest."

This book is an attempt to begin that protest. Yale law professor

Akhil Amar has described the ideal role of a legislature as akin to that of a jury in a public trial—a diverse group of people coming together as a single entity to consider all the relevant facts, to gather information, weigh the evidence, and discuss among themselves the best recourse. For any American interested in justice, the rights of the individual, and the collective good of the community, it is impossible to imagine a trial in which members of the jury were divided according to which political club they belonged to, with a majority representing whichever club won the greater number of votes in the last round of elections. As a free people, we would never countenance such a partisan decision in a case of robbery or libel or fraud, but we willingly accept it for the much bigger jury that decides whether our sons and daughters will be sent off to fight and die in foreign wars, whether we should continue to fund an emergency response agency, or whether we should ensure that the medicines sold in our pharmacies are safe. Having political parties—that is, having Americans—gather together to support common goals is an essential ingredient of the democratic process, but allowing them to also dictate how we elect our officials and how we govern our nation is an unfathomable surrender of our rights as a people to decide how we will be governed. Amar tells his students that this America we live in was the first nation in all of history to allow the people themselves to decide how they would be governed. It is one of the most important achievements in the history of mankind, and the power we have surrendered to private political clubs is stealing that wonderful gift from us.

SEVEN

Debate and Democracy

Step Six: Restore Democracy to Congress

The United States House of Representatives does not operate according to *Robert's Rules of Order*. It adopts its own rules, and one of them allows the Rules Committee, heavily dominated by the majority party, to determine which bills can be brought before the entire House for consideration and what amendments, if any, can be debated. No matter how many members of the minority party may support a proposal—fifty, eighty, one hundred, two hundred—the majority can simply refuse to let the bill be considered. If the majority brings a bill to the floor, the minority can be prevented from even attempting to amend it. Here's how:

If a bill is brought to the floor under an "open" rule, debate is free-flowing and there is no restriction on the ability of members to propose changes in the legislation under consideration. If the Rules Committee presents a "modified open" rule, only a limited number of amendments are permitted; those that are to be considered are specifically identified, and time for their consideration is strictly limited. Under a "closed" rule, House members are given the option of voting for or against the legislation, but without any opportunity to offer improvements or changes. In their book *Managing Uncertainty in the House of Representatives*, political scientists Stanley Bach and Steven S. Smith noted that in the 94th Congress (1974–76), 84.3 percent of all bills were brought to the House floor under an open rule.[1] A decade later, that percentage was down to 55.4 percent. Yet even that is misleading: on the most important and controversial issues in the 94th Congress, 63.6 percent were considered under open rules that allowed for full debate and possible amendment; that number was 70.6 percent in the 95th Congress (my first as a member of the House of Representatives). By the 99th Congress (1985–86) only 13.6 percent of the most important legislation was considered under an open rule that permitted true deliberation. Systematically, partisan considerations had moved to the fore, and real consideration of legislative alternatives was being eradicated from the "peoples' house" of the federal government. And it got even worse: according to a report by the House Rules Committee, there was not a single bill considered under open rule in the 111th Congress (2009–10). The report noted that 27 percent of the House members in the 112th Congress had never experienced consideration of legislation brought to the floor under an open rule.[2]

This phenomenon—the use of raw power to stifle opposition—is not the work of one political party. In his study of House rules over three successive Congresses, two in which Democrats were in charge and one under Republican leadership, Don Wolfensberger of the Woodrow Wilson Center wrote in December 2010: "When they [House Democrats] took power, the new majority proceeded to endorse the more partisan processes followed by her [Nancy Pelosi's] predecessor," including "marginalization of the minority."[3] Wolfensberger noted that in the two Congresses in which Democrats were in control, they restricted the ability of Republicans to offer amendments on 86 percent of all bills considered by the House in one Congress and in 99 percent in the other. For the Republican-controlled session that Wolfensberger studied, the figure was 81 percent. "Democrats," he concluded, "have become worse than Republicans were at their worst." This is quite a standard: in even the best of the three cases, free and open discussion and serious consideration of alternatives were permitted on fewer than one bill in five! Year after year, no matter who is in charge, the leaders of our Congress are choking off debate and undermining the single most important feature of a democratic government—the ability to freely weigh options and to choose among them. In a true democracy, dissent is cherished; in today's Congress, it is crushed.

That is not to say that members of Congress lack a sense of irony. Wolfensberger, writing in *Roll Call*, pointed out that the day after parliamentarians Johnson and McKay spoke at the Wilson Center about the concentration of power in the House leadership, Rules Committee Republicans charged Democrats with having "pursued their agenda at the expense of the House as a basic institution of our democracy" and having "engineered the exclusion of opposing viewpoints." Apparently stifling dissent is acceptable if it's done on only 81 percent of bills considered. The next day, the new House Speaker, Republican John Boehner, speaking at the American Enterprise Institute, called for allowing more amendments. "We should open things up and let the battle of ideas help break down the scar tissue between the two parties . . . let's give [Members] a chance to do their jobs. Let's let legislators legislate again."[4] Boehner argued that "the true test is whether our ideas, policies and values are able to stand the test of a fair debate and a fair vote." One would think that this idea might have occurred to both parties sooner. But while

Boehner did make an effort to open the process a bit more, those restrictive "closed" rules and semiclosed rules continued to be standard fare, though not as frequently, under his watch.

If discussion was freer, if debate was encouraged, and if multiple proposals to solve the nation's problems were given fair consideration, Congress would additionally receive some important side benefits. "The refreshing benefits of such a change," Wolfensberger wrote, "would be not only the re-engagement of Members in constructive policymaking but the enlightenment of the people about the policy issues involved—something lost in rushing through thousand-page bills with little debate or amendment." Another benefit would be "a lot less fighting between the parties over unfair procedures."

For many years, students of American government accepted the notion that the House of Representatives, with its two-year terms and great susceptibility to public moods, would necessarily be the congressional chamber in which partisanship was more prevalent. Senators, protected by their six-year terms, would have greater freedom to reflect and, when called for, stand up against the tide of public opinion. The Senate, in George Washington's famous analogy, would be the saucer in which the hot tea of partisan division would have a chance to cool. Until relatively recently the Senate included many members who had bypassed the crucible of the partisan conflicts that were so prevalent in the House; instead they arrived in Washington after serving as governors or in other statewide or federal administrative positions in which the primary emphasis was on management. Not any longer. In *Party Polarization in Congress*, Sean Theriault described how polarization in the House spread to the Senate as more and more House members ran for the Senate and won, taking their partisan tendencies with them.[5] Republicans who had taken part in Gingrich-era parliamentary warfare—Jon Kyl of Arizona; Rick Santorum of Pennsylvania; Jim Inhofe of Oklahoma; George Allen of Virginia; and Jim Bunning of Kentucky—

moved over to the Senate. Doing the same were Democrats like Barbara Boxer of California; Dick Durbin of Illinois; Chuck Schumer of New York, and Sherrod Brown of Ohio. With their commitment to lockstep party conformity and bomb-throwing conflict, senators began to lose their "cooling saucer" identity and became much like a second House.

In the Senate, individual members have a much greater opportunity to be heard—there is no "rules" committee, at least none with similar authority—but various tactics have been employed to shut down democratic governance in that chamber as well. Individual senators, for example, may halt consideration of appointments simply by placing a "hold" on some future action. The hold is a tactic that flows from the Senate's practice of moving legislation forward by unanimous consent—which, when withheld, can often stop a proposed action in its tracks. It is easy enough to see why the practice began: in a deliberative democracy, it is sometimes important to slow the train, to allow more time to gather information and examine arguments. But the practice has crossed the boundaries of necessity and has become a tool for thwarting the democratic process.

That has been the case, too, with the filibuster, a provision in Senate rules that was originally created to give individual senators an opportunity to force extended consideration of proposals that would bring about significant change. That the filibuster can be an important tool for the triumph of good over evil was well captured in the 1939 Frank Capra film *Mr. Smith Goes to Washington*, in which Jimmy Stewart plays a naïve young senator who is falsely accused of corruption (by fellow senators who are themselves corrupt) and saves himself from expulsion and humiliation by use of the filibuster, a rule that allows any senator to control the Senate's time for as long as he or she chooses to speak.

But the filibuster was not an easy thing to use. It required the senator who used it to demonstrate a belief in the issue's importance by remaining on the Senate floor, speaking continuously. While Jimmy Stewart's filibuster was fictional, New York Senator Alfonse D'Amato's was not. D'Amato was known as "Senator Pothole" for his commitment to issues of benefit to his own constituents. In 1986, trying to forestall debate on a bill that would cut funding for a trainer aircraft built in New York, he spoke for more than twenty-three straight hours. A few years later, on a bill of slightly less consequence, he spoke for fifteen hours, preventing the Senate from conducting any business while he entertained visitors in the gallery with a rendition of the 1939 song "South of the Border (Down Mexico Way)." Louisiana Senator Huey Long did almost as well in 1935, when he held the floor for nearly fifteen hours, filling the time by reciting recipes for fried oysters and turnip green pot liquor. The all-time filibuster champion, however, was South Carolina's Strom Thurmond, who read the Declaration of Independence, the Bill of Rights, and even George Washington's Farewell Address during the twenty-four hours and eighteen minutes he held the floor. Ironically, he recited the Bill of Rights in an attempt to prevent the Senate from acting to pass civil rights legislation. Others also filibustered at length and in person, standing on the Senate floor: Wayne Morse of Oregon for nearly twenty-two and a half hours in 1953, Robert LaFollette, Sr., of Wisconsin for nearly eighteen and a half hours in 1908, and William Proxmire, also of Wisconsin, for more than sixteen hours in 1981. In 1957 a group of senators, occupying the floor by serially yielding time to each other, brought the Senate's proceedings to a halt by talking nonstop for nearly two months. Amazingly, today, without the theatrics, it has gotten even worse.

Senators were generally reluctant to invoke cloture (that is, vote to set a time limit on a filibuster) because the same right to speak that Strom Thurmond, Huey Long, Al D'Amato, and others employed was one that they might someday claim for themselves if they felt equally passionate about an issue before the Senate. In addition, they felt that by tolerating filibusters they were demonstrating their commitment to free speech and a slow, deliberate governing process. Therefore they simply waited out the talkers, who might be able to go on for a long time, but not forever. Between 1927 and 1962, the Senate tried eleven separate times to shut off filibusters and failed each time. Then, in 1975, a rule change reduced the number of votes required to shut off debate from two-thirds of the senators present—sixty-seven if all were present—to sixty, regardless of how many were present—a change that should have made it easier to stop the talking and resume business. But the same change also eliminated the requirement that the senator doing the filibustering must actually occupy the floor. Now a senator who wishes to filibuster a bill need not even appear in the Senate at all. Merely informing the majority leader of one's "intent" to filibuster is sufficient, and the senator who would have otherwise insisted on talking agrees to let the Senate proceed with its other business. As a result, the Senate does not grind to a halt, but it does put off action on the targeted legislation.

In the hyperpartisan warfare that increasingly holds the Congress captive, a minority party now need have only forty-one seats in the Senate to prevent the majority from acting. And it does so without a single senator having to strain his or her vocal chords or skip a meal. Banding together as a partisan bloc, a minority of senators are able to kill legislation not only by the use of the filibuster but by the mere threat of using it. Republican Senator Scott Brown's surprise victory in Massachusetts in 2010 became a seminal event because it elevated his party's numbers in the Senate from forty, a position of almost complete powerlessness, to forty-one—at which point Republicans, outnumbered by eighteen votes (59–41) nonetheless could block almost anything the majority wanted to do, simply by threatening to filibuster as a partisan bloc.

There is a valid case to be made for the filibuster. If, for example, a majority signed on to a proposal to grant powers to the president that properly reside with the Congress, or to limit authority that now rests with the states, or if a majority proposed some other fundamental change that might properly require senators to block further action, the filibuster would be a means of bringing to the legislative process one of the underlying premises of American democracy—the protection of minority rights even against a temporary majority. But it is a tool to be used sparingly, not as a legislative maneuver to preclude an elected majority from doing anything a minority might oppose. Today, however, as John Avlon has pointed out on the website Daily Beast, the filibuster is "invoked more than ever before— from roughly one a year between 1920 and 1970 to an average of 70 times a year now."⁶ Avlon quotes Tennessee Congressman Jim Cooper (who, with Avlon and myself, is a cofounder of the No Labels reform group) on the difference between today's filibusters and those of the past: "Back in the 1960s," Cooper points out, "Strom Thurmond had to risk his bladder to filibuster; now no Senator has skin in the game. They just ask a staffer to file paperwork." The filibuster, Avlon observed, "has gone from a rare physical endurance test to a routine parliamentary maneuver." Requiring senators to actually filibuster in person, he says, would make the tactic "a special occasion rather than a first reflex."

So consider just these four examples, two in each chamber: in the House of Representatives, the majority can block legislation from even being considered and can use "closed rules" to prohibit any attempt to revise bills the majority favors, essentially excluding the minority almost entirely from the governing process; in the Senate, the minority can use holds and filibusters to prevent any action it opposes. In both cases, democracy is stymied; party discipline prevails and the deliberative, democratic process is the victim.

Again, it doesn't have to be this way.

Let's begin with the Senate. One can justify the use of a hold to prevent Senate leaders from ramming presidential appointments through that body without allowing sufficient time for investigation of the appointee's qualifications or positions—completely legitimate avenues for Senate inquiry—but the process should be open and public. The Senate has ostensibly moved to eliminate the wall of secrecy behind which holds have been placed, but it has actually done no such thing. Today each hold is ascribed to an actual senator, but in the arcane way the Senate does things the instigator of the hold may still remain anonymous. For example, a Republican senator who wishes his or her action to remain undisclosed may simply ask a party leader—Minority Leader Mitch McConnell, perhaps—to allow the hold to be placed under McConnell's name. There are two things wrong with this practice: first, it prevents the public from knowing who is responsible when a legislative action or a federal appointment is blocked; second and equally important, it prevents the public from knowing why it is being blocked. Senate rules should require disclosure of the name of the senator who actually requests a hold on a Senate action.

The second problem is the singularity of the action. In today's Senate a senator may block the confirmation of a deputy assistant secretary of agriculture because of unhappiness with the administration's plans to discontinue a constituent company's contract to provide shoes to the navy. The Senate's rules should be changed to prohibit holds that are not directly relevant to the action being blocked; there must be a legitimate nonparochial issue of national interest at stake. In addition, for any hold to take effect, the rules should require that it be supported publicly by at least three additional senators, who would also be named and whose reasons for joining in the action would also be made public. These changes would retain the legitimate purposes of a hold while preventing any senator's personal pout from prevailing over Congress's need to perform its constitutional duties.

Holds are not all about individual senators exploiting the rules for personal purposes. The hold has had another, and even more disturbing, use as well: as a partisan tool to block the Senate majority from acting, while saving the minority from having to engage in a serious debate. These proposed changes would permit legitimate delays but prevent both personal pique and party posturing from impeding the Senate's work.

Like the hold, the filibuster has a legitimate purpose in preventing the majority from steamrolling the minority. But when forty-one senators become a de facto majority, standing together to prevent the actual elected majority from passing any serious legislation, that purpose has been turned on its head. The filibuster has been transformed in this new superpartisan world into a weapon of tyranny by the minority. One purpose of elections is to determine whose policies shall prevail so long as they remain within the permissible boundaries set by the Constitution. If voters have sent fifty-five members of Party A to the Senate and only forty-five of Party B, one would hope the two parties, with divergent policies and priorities, would seek areas of common ground; but if common ground is not found, it is the views of the fifty-five, not the forty-five, that should prevail until there is another election.

The question then becomes how to retain the filibuster, with its legitimate purposes, and yet prevent a minority from abusing it. Here, two rules changes would be beneficial. The first is to eliminate the "remote" filibuster. The majority, however pragmatically it may wish to move on to other business, should no longer capitulate to threats of a filibuster. Instead, senators who warn of a filibuster should be required to actually take the Senate floor and hold it for as long as they can. But the rules should also be changed to require that the filibustering senator not read pot liquor recipes or passages from Murakami or Longfellow, but speak to the legislation that he or she is attempting to block. House rules require amendments to actually be germane to the purpose of the bill being considered; the Senate likewise should require comments during a filibuster to be germane to the issue being filibustered. To prevent D'Amato filibusters (on an issue that stirs the passion of only one senator), they should require at least half a dozen cosponsors, each of whom would be required to participate in holding the Senate floor. In the age of televised House and Senate proceedings, all will be out in the open, the filibuster's supporters and their arguments will be fully exposed, and it will be up to the people, weighing what they see and hear, to convey their support or opposition to the rest of the Senate.

Finally, the Senate should change the rules for invoking cloture. Instead of allowing the filibuster to be cut off with sixty votes, require sixty-seven—for the first three days; sixty votes until the seventh day; fifty-eight after the seventh day; fifty-five after the tenth day; fifty after twelve days. As time passes, ending filibusters should become easier, but those supporting them will have been allowed more than ample time to make their arguments to scholars, editorial writers, voters, and their Senate colleagues. Allow a filibuster's supporters a full and fair opportunity to make their case, to try to win public support—and then let the results fall where they will. Instead of allowing this powerful weapon to be used as a partisan strategy to block democracy, turn it instead into a tool to strengthen the democratic process.

Which leaves the House of Representatives, with the majority's ability to block bills and amendments from consideration, yet to be dealt with.

On most committees in the House of Representatives, membership is divided between the parties in more or less the same ratio as that which the two parties enjoy in the House itself, although it is not uncommon for the majority party—which writes the rules—to give itself an extra seat or two on those committees in which issues important to the leadership and central to the party agenda are to be decided (a tactic whose underlying assumption is that the party's appointments to the committee will not think for themselves). The House Rules Committee is a different matter; when it comes to partisan stacking of the deck, the Rules Committee has no equal in either house of Congress and perhaps in no other presumably democratic forum.

The Rules Committee is often described in political science textbooks as the "traffic cop" of the House. This description seems almost benign—traffic cops, after all, make sure the rules are being followed, but they don't write the rules, and they certainly don't write the rules to gain some personal advantage. But seats on the Rules Committee—and especially the committee's chairmanship—are among the most powerful positions in the entire Congress, House or Senate. Nothing goes to the House floor without the permission of the Rules Committee. If a bill is reported favorably out of an authorizing committee—for parks, highways, tanks, battleships, schools, health care, or retirement subsidies—it goes no further toward becoming law unless the Rules Committee says it can. That is why the committee's small hearing room in an upper floor of the Capitol is often crowded with powerful committee chairs making their case for the rules under which their bills will be voted on (whether amendments will be permitted, whether the bill will be debated for days or only a few hours, and whether it can include provisions that are not technically germane to the rest of the bill). If the committee chooses to let legislation go forward under an open rule, those questions answer themselves. In such a case, any member can offer any amendment, speak on its behalf, and ask for a vote, whether the majority favors it or not. But the committee can also preclude amendments altogether, no matter how many members support them. The committee's power to move bills to the floor under a closed rule was designed to permit the House to act swiftly on urgent or noncontroversial legislation and to prevent a small number of obstructionists from interfering with a bill's passage by offering dozens of amendments that were irrelevant or had little support. But that's not how the power is generally used. The Rules Committee is not a traffic cop, it's the Speaker's private gang, with the chair and all of the majority party's members selected by, and answerable to, the Speaker, and all-powerful in determining what legislation may even be considered for passage. In this sense, what happens on the House floor is not democracy but dictatorship, no matter which political party is in control. The process is designed not for deliberation but to allow the majority party to work its will on the government without consideration of other points of view.

It may appear at first glance that "a majority working its will" is also working the public's will. After all, that party gained the majority because more citizens voted for its candidates than for the candidates of the other party. But that overlooks two significant factors. The first, as described in the discussion of gerrymandered congressional districts, is that partisan redistricting can create an election in which more of a state's voters choose candidates from Party A, yet Party B winds up with more of the state's congressional seats. So the congressional majority that can use House rules to exercise almost dictatorial power may in fact represent a minority of the actual votes cast in the most recent election.

But it is also wrong to assume that, even if Party A received more votes, the voters who cast them would necessarily oppose amendments the party's leaders were trying to block. Because President Ronald Reagan was particularly adept at communication with voters, the Democratic Party leadership, especially when Jim Wright of Texas was Speaker, feared that if a Reagan-backed amendment were allowed to come up for a vote, many Democrats might find themselves under intense pressure from their constituents to support it. That explains why, during the Wright speakership, the number of closed rules soared. The same dynamic could have played out during Bill Clinton's presidency when it overlapped with Republican control of Congress. Precluding amendments as a legislative strategy puts partisan control ahead of the public's desires.

The great power of the Rules Committee has led to some of the most egregious abuses of the legislative process and has fueled some of the most bitter partisan warfare in the House of Representatives. It has also greatly increased the ability of party leaders to demand absolute fealty from members of their team. When a House Speaker appoints his or her party's representatives to the Rules Committee, they are expected to follow the Speaker's directions as to what bills may be allowed on the floor and what amendments, if any, may be considered. The leader of the minority party determines who will represent that group on the committee, and they too are essentially arms of the leadership, but the Speaker's side always wins, because even when the House membership is almost evenly divided, the majority party nevertheless gives itself a significant majority on the Rules Committee. Most observers may view the committee's decisions as strictly procedural but their impact is enormous and often determinative of the outcome on important policy debates. The failure of even experienced Congress-watchers to appreciate the impact of the committee's decisions has led some members from districts that are either more conservative or more liberal than the member's party to adopt a clever but deceitful strategy: ultimately voting *against* their party's legislation when it comes up for a vote, in order to satisfy their constituents, but only after first voting *for* the restrictive rule that virtually ensures the bill's passage. As a result, these members get to have their cake and eat it, too, because the chances are slim that their constituents will catch on to what they have done.

Battles over approval of the rule for consideration of a bill not only have served as a focal point for fierce partisan struggle but have also bred simmering resentments that undermine any tendency to view members of the opposition party as potential legislative partners. Newt Gingrich's rise to power can be traced directly to the numerous "closed rules" imposed under the speakership of Jim Wright, causing even moderate Republicans, who wanted the opportunity to play a role in the congressional debates, to turn to the most fiercely partisan champion they could find on the assumption that he would fight for their right to have their bills and amendments considered. Political scientist Sean Theriault attributes much of the increase in congressional polarization to the votes on these procedural issues.

There is a simple way around this dilemma, even if one were to grant that party leaders are not trying to gain advantage for their agenda priorities but merely trying to keep bills from becoming bogged down by a stream of amendments. Even when major bills were subjected to dozens of amendments, and passage might take four or five long days of debate and votes, that was still a small price to pay to prevent transforming "the world's greatest deliberative body" into one of the least democratic. But those, as always, are not the only options.

First, the House should make the Rules Committee a true traffic cop, with no partisan advantage whatsoever. I proposed above that membership on lawmaking and spending committees should eschew partisan division, but the Rules Committee, which determines what may or may not happen to a proposal, should not be nonpartisan, like the rest, but bipartisan, with both political parties equally represented.

If one wishes to honor the democratic necessity of considering alternatives, the best way to accomplish that goal is to guarantee that any serious amendment will receive a hearing and a vote, but that amendments that are merely dilatory will be precluded. How would that distinction be made, given that the seriousness of a proposal is often in the eye of the beholder? Here's one way to do it. The House would achieve both of its purposes—a more democratic process and avoidance of deliberate stalling gambits—by providing that any amendment that has at least one hundred cosponsors—nearly one-fourth of the entire House—would be permitted a hearing, with supporting witnesses, in committee, where the public record is made, and then a full and open discussion and a recorded vote on the House floor. The process would be much more democratic, allowing honest consideration of policy alternatives, which is the legislative feature that distinguishes democracies from dictatorships.

Ensuring consideration of nontrivial legislation even when offered by members of the minority party would break the majority's ability to essentially gag the opposition and freeze out of the legislative process the elected representatives of tens of millions of Americans. It would restore the constitutional intent of letting the people, through their elected representatives, decide the fate of the nation. Defenders of the congressional status quo have argued, correctly, that an institution like the U.S. Congress cannot reasonably be expected to function as a pure democracy, that it requires structure and empowered leadership, and clear and comprehensive rules. After all, they argue, if every bill or amendment that any member of Congress wanted to bring forward were given sufficient time for debate and a recorded vote, nothing would ever get done. The nation's founders deliberately established a process that would be slow, but not one that could not function. Those caveats must be taken seriously. The proposals I have offered here would maintain all the necessary congressional structure—there would be a Speaker of the House and a leader in the Senate, and the authorizing and appropriating committees would continue to hear witnesses and recommend or not recommend the adoption of proposed laws. The House would retain its Rules Committee. Both the House and Senate would maintain their rules for debate and voting. But the system would no longer be based on an artificial division between rival political clubs.

EIGHT

Rearrange the Furniture

Step Seven: Eliminate the Trappings of Partisanship

For readers who have not yet visited the national Capitol and seen the impressive chambers in which the Senate and House of Representatives conduct their business, let me offer a brief tour. (And for those of you who already have been there, let me point out a few things you may have overlooked.)

First, the legislative process begins not in the ornate chambers of the Capitol building itself but rather in the committee and subcommittee hearing rooms that are scattered throughout the six congressional office buildings (three for the House, three for the Senate). So let's begin there. Let's walk into a hearing room while the committee is meeting, listening to the opinions of an expert witness, and take a seat facing the front of the room, looking directly at the members who are charged with writing our nation's laws.

We can ignore the witnesses and the table at which they sit (for our purpose they are beside the point, other than that most of them will be presenting the very assessment that the members of the majority party want to hear and to have made a part of the record supporting their proposed action). The people who really matter are the legislators themselves. If you know which ones are the Republicans and which are the Democrats, you will immediately see that there is no randomness to the seating: to your left (to the right of the committee chair, who sits in the middle) you will see only Democrats; to your right, only Republicans. Even though this is the United States Congress, not a party caucus, and we are ostensibly a single nation, the committee's Democrats and Republicans are not interspersed. Seating is by seniority (the newest member of the committee is seated farthest from the chair and is the last to be called upon to ask questions or make statements), but in fact there are two separate seniorities—one within the majority party and one within the minority. It is as though these members of Congress seated before you are actually members of two separate entities, seated not at one table but at two that have been glued together.

In the course of the hearing, you'll notice that some of the committee members may occasionally get up and leave the hearing room through one of two side doors, each of which leads to an adjacent room where they can make phone calls or meet with staff members. Or they can simply pass through to another door that enables them to leave the hearing altogether. But you'll also notice that some of the committee members will go out one door and that others will leave through another door at the opposite end of the long committee table. That is because, even though we tend to see them all as members of the same committee, they actually see themselves as either the Republican members or the Democratic members, and each party has its own separate side room, with the rooms divided by the full width of the hearing room.

Having observed this strange bifurcation, you will not then be surprised to go to the Capitol and take a seat in the galleries that overlook the House and Senate chambers as the members engage in debate. Both of these chambers are opulent with ample marble and carved wood, as befits a great nation. But there is also something disconcerting about the scenes we will witness. One might expect the House chamber to be the forum for a single entity, the United States House of Representatives: one body, part of one government, all its members having taken one oath of office. But if you recognize the members by sight, and know which parties they belong to, you will quickly observe that on one side of the chamber, to your right, there are only Republicans; on the other, separated from the Republicans by an aisle wide enough for two people to walk through side by side, sit the Democrats. Perhaps one or two members will have crossed that aisle to chat with somebody from "the other side," but for the most part the aisle is like an ocean separating two continents.

Senators address their colleagues while standing at their desks, but in the House, as a debate continues, you will observe something strange. When a Democrat is called upon to address the chamber, he or she will walk to a lectern situated not in the center of the front space ("the well" of the House) but set off to the left of center (from your perspective, looking down and toward the Speaker's chair). When a Republican is recognized to speak, he or she will use a different lectern, set to the right of the center. It is as if members of each party were afraid of getting cooties if they touched a surface that had previously been touched by a member of the other party. The first time I gave a speech on the House floor, early in my first term, I did not understand this rule of separateness; I naïvely began to speak from the "wrong" lectern and was quickly admonished—by members of both parties—to move over to the lectern designated for members of my own party. I have often told this story when taking visitors to the House floor and have always framed it as a moment of personal embarrassment. But it is the Congress that should be embarrassed. If this Congress is of our country, writing our laws, under our Constitution, why does it operate as though it were not one body but two completely separate Congresses, each with its own place for its members to sit, to stand, to speak, according to which private club they belong to?

Picture an ancient battlefield. As the opposing armies face each other across a dividing space, the generals who command them sit behind the lines, each group of commanders ensconced behind its own ranks of soldiers. Similarly, in the House chamber, there are separate leadership tables, one on each side of that wide center-aisle divide. These congressional "generals" and their rank-and-file troops can conduct research on how other members have voted by using taxpayer-provided computers, but each side has its own computers, one at the generals' table, which is near the front of the chamber, and another located near the back of that army's embankment of seats. Behind each encampment, off to the side, are the cloakrooms where House members who are temporarily not engaged in the debate gather to eat, read newspapers, watch television, make telephone calls, or talk to each other. Republicans have their room, Democrats have theirs. Not only do they not sit together in the debating hall, they don't even slurp soup together. A representative is not legally prohibited from entering the other team's inner sanctum, but if you do, as I sometimes did, you may feel as though you've walked in on a drug deal or a tryst. You will know—even though nothing will be said—that you have strayed into a place where you do not belong . . . even though these are your fellow members of the United States Congress.

And finally, each party's leadership maintains a small office opening onto the House floor; they are, of course, separate offices, on opposite sides of the chamber.

Now let's move across to the Senate side of the Capitol and take a look. Whereas House members, given their larger numbers, sit in rows of seats, as though in a theater, each senator has his or her own desk. Seating is arranged by seniority, with the party leaders in the front and others seated ever farther toward the back as their seniority diminishes. While I have referred to the Congress as a whole as the world's "greatest deliberative body," this is a title the Senate prefers to keep for itself. The Senate's rules provide greater latitude for its members; rules are fewer and deference is expected. Yet here, too, the architecture tells a different story. Here, too, there is an aisle like an ocean, with Democrats all seated along one coast and Republicans along the other.

Advocates of dressing school-age children in look-alike uniforms make two claims for such a practice: one is that it reduces distinction (if all girls in a class are dressed alike, it is not easy to distinguish the wealthier from the less wealthy, thus reducing the sense of privilege for one and the feeling of being second-class for the other); the other is that being in uniform stokes one's sense of pride and improves one's behavior and, perhaps, the ability to learn. The Senate claims all members of that body are like the children in uniform— peers, equals, a collective. But while senators may be figuratively indistinguishable (the men do dress very much alike), and the Senate's rules somewhat lessen the inferior status that members of the House's minority might feel, the very division of the chamber makes it clear that this is not one collective but two, each huddled on its gang's turf. Here, too, the members of one party sit to one side of the center aisle, the members of the other party to the other side. The separateness is visibly reinforced every time the Senate convenes.

Imagine a psychiatrist who has been called in to counsel a family in which communication had broken down. The first thing the psychiatrist might do is to suggest rearranging the furniture. "Conversation circles" are called that because they encourage conversation: sofas and chairs face each other; the potato chips are on a table in the center so that anyone who reaches for a chip must lean toward another family member. The separateness is eliminated. Gradually, rules may emerge regarding how much time family members may spend on independent (exclusionary) activities, while the general focus turns toward the inclusionary and interactive events that allow individuals to function as members of a common entity working toward common goals.

One small step toward unraveling the partisanship that is destroying the ability of our legislators to cooperate across the aisle might be simply to rearrange the furniture—not to work across the aisle but to eliminate the aisle altogether. In the Senate's chamber, we could arrange seating solely by seniority within the institution, not within the party; let members of Team A sit beside members of Team B if that's where their seniority places them (as it often will).

Let's rearrange the leaders' seating, too. Let the leaders of each team sit beside each other, not at opposite ends of a great divide. In the absence of the vice president and the Senate's president pro tempore, the chairmanship of the day (or for a particular debate) falls to a designated member of the majority party. But if the purpose is to ensure proper debate and adherence to Senate rules and to provide orderly discussion, it should make no difference which of the two political clubs the day's chair belongs to: rotate the chairmanship among all members of the Senate.

In the House, do the same. End the practice of separate lecterns; place a single lectern dead-center in the front of the chamber; end the habit of seating according to party affiliation; make both cloakrooms available to any House member who wishes to use them; make the computers accessible to all. The Speaker presides only when the House is in the final process of approving legislation that has already been debated and amended; during the debate-and-amendment period, when the House adopts the useful fiction that it is merely operating as a committee ("the committee of the whole," to get around the constitutional requirements for a quorum), a member selected by the Speaker presides as "chair." But because it is really the parliamentarian who rules on the appropriateness of a member's comments or on attempts to introduce an amendment, it is of no consequence to which party the chairperson belongs. That position, too, should be filled on a rotating basis.

We have partisanship, incivility, unwillingness to compromise because our system itself is designed to encourage conflict. Democracies require vigorous debate and serious consideration of alternatives. In a democracy, conflicts will naturally arise, and as a diverse nation we should celebrate these struggles and the fact that we have the freedom to engage in such strenuous debate. But the system in which we have wrapped our democracy engenders conflict over party label, over which club one belongs to, over who might gain an advantage in the next election. That does not celebrate democracy, it destroys it. Rearranging the furniture will not in itself change the party-label fixation that has done so much harm to our collective well-being, but it's a start.

NINE

Rivals, Not Enemies

Step Eight: Longer Workweeks, More Interaction

Every two years, at the beginning of each new Congress, the Congressional Management Foundation (CMF) produces a "management guide" for the new members of the House and Senate. For the most part, the guide deals with the mundane but vital details of establishing a congressional office and building an effective career in public office. Various chapters offer advice on hiring new staff members, determining which committee assignments to pursue, how to make the best use of the available technology, and how to create an office budget. But Brad Fitch, the Foundation's president, knows the Congress as it actually operates. So CMF's guide for the 112th Congress included a special section titled "Increased Partisanship and Lack of Civility." In other words, new members of Congress, welcome to your new world.[1]

"In both chambers," the guide states, "factions or the minority party leadership have occasionally used protest votes and other tactics to shut down the floor for a time. Tensions have run high as leaders lob charges of obstructionism at each other in the media. In the House, vigorous debate has occasionally escalated into instances of name-calling, and in one or two high profile cases, near fist-fights." The guide then quotes a *Washington Post* article from June 2000 (clear evidence that the rancor that now plagues the Congress is not a short-term phenomenon), stating that "three weeks after the partisan warfare threatened a legislative meltdown, the Senate has stepped back from the brink, pulled itself together and worked its way through two virtually glitch-free weeks. But the fundamental problems that caused a virtual shutdown of Senate business before the Memorial Day recess—including policy disputes, personal tensions, power struggles and the pressure-cooker atmosphere of an election year—remain as threatening as ever. They lurk just beneath the surface, ready to explode again when a new provocation occurs."

No Labels, the bipartisan reform group formed in Washington, DC, in 2011, has suggested several nonlegislative steps to ease the incivility that makes it even harder to form across-the-aisle agreements, including longer in-Washington workweeks, monthly bipartisan gatherings ("without cameras or interest groups"), and elimination of partisan seating in the House and Senate chambers. The Congressional Management Foundation has made a number of other suggestions over the years that have been endorsed by a variety of political observers.

It's a sad thing that many of the best-intentioned reforms turn out to be counterproductive. One of the worst was an insistence that members of Congress stop traveling overseas. The impetus for the reform was a pattern of abuse by a few members who saw the House's willingness to pay for foreign trips as an opportunity for taxpayer-funded junkets, complete with golf outings, shopping sprees, and tourism. Pictures of congressmen on island beaches stirred a predictable reaction among the taxpayers who had paid for those trips.

Unfortunately, instead of creating regulations to govern what was and was not permissible on such trips, reformers demanded that they be ended altogether.

The overseas travel restriction had two deleterious effects. The first was that members of Congress—the men and women with the final say on treaties, trade, foreign aid, and war and peace—became reluctant to travel abroad. They stayed home and got their information from newspapers and television reports, or they heard only whatever members of the executive branch wanted to tell them. Meanwhile, presidents, Cabinet members, and agency directors routinely attend overseas conferences on climate, nuclear security, property rights, and other issues. This disparity in information gathering strengthens the executive branch and weakens the legislative branch, which constitutionally has the greatest need for the information because it is supposed to write the laws, serve as a check on the executive, oversee compliance with the laws it has enacted, and monitor the spending of the money it has appropriated. (For example, when I was the ranking member of the House Subcommittee on Foreign Operations, I visited the headquarters of the International Fund for Agricultural Development and, based on what I learned during this trip, cut a million dollars of taxpayer money from the United States' contribution to the organization.)

The second result was more subtle but, in terms of the current partisan excesses, no less important. Let me illustrate by first introducing you to a former colleague, David Obey of Wisconsin. As you know, I'm a Republican. Dave Obey is a Democrat—a quite liberal Democrat, and someone who is passionate and outspoken about his beliefs. Dave is also (and I'll bet he'd not contest the description) an often prickly sort, perhaps because he holds his views so strongly. Before he became the chair of the House Appropriations Committee, Dave chaired the foreign operations subcommittee, and I was the minority party's ranking member. Needless to say, there were many times when Dave and I did not agree. On one occasion, another Republican, Jerry Lewis of California, tried to offer an amendment that Dave and I both opposed. Obey declared that he would not permit Lewis to offer the amendment. Even though I, too, would vote against the amendment—which was almost certain to fail in any event—I objected. From my standpoint, we in the minority could not permit the chair to simply prohibit one of our members from even offering an amendment for consideration. Dave would not relent and I then led the Republican members of the subcommittee in a walkout, explaining that we would return to the table when he changed his mind—as he did, days later, after many angry phone calls to my office.

But here's the thing: as the chair and ranking minority member of the foreign operations subcommittee, respectively, Dave Obey and I had important responsibilities. Our subcommittee disbursed more than $20 billion a year for everything from human rights training to the development of overseas markets for American products. To meet those responsibilities and to ensure that we were able to make the best decisions possible, we not only questioned the American officials overseeing the programs we funded, we called on the foreign government agencies and individuals who were responsible for implementing the programs we supported and the expenditure of American tax dollars. Traveling together, Dave and I found many opportunities to talk, and we discovered that we were both committed to doing what we thought best for the welfare of the United States. I also learned that Dave Obey is in fact a Wisconsin transplant; he is actually a fellow Oklahoman, born in the small town of Okmulgee, not far from where folksinger Woody Guthrie was born. In fact, Dave was a musician himself: he and his wife, Joan, and their children played the harmonica and made recordings together. It was also obvious that their love for America was as deep as that of anybody on my side of the aisle. Dave was not an enemy, just another devoted American whose experiences and education had led him to different conclusions than mine as to what policies would best achieve the goals we both desired. There is no magical Hollywood ending to this tale—Dave and I continued to disagree on many things—but we also worked harder to seek ways in which we could find agreement, and ways in which we could work together harmoniously even when agreement eluded us. Long after we had finished our service in the House together, with nothing to be gained by "cooperation" or even continued contact, Dave called to ask whether I would join him in a presentation he had been asked to make.

I've been asked why this matters. How does getting to know a fellow member contribute to civility and better problem-solving? Try this experiment: consider getting acquainted with somebody you know only casually and simply haven't liked—and perhaps have even said unkind things about. This could be someone at work, in your church or synagogue, or in any other place where you may know each other only in passing or in the occasional meeting, and about whom you know nothing more personal than the color of his tie, or her hairstyle. Perhaps this person is somebody you've never really met at all, never been in a meeting with, but about whom you've heard enough to form an opinion. Invite that person to join you for coffee. Ask where he or she grew up. Ask about children. In other words, have a chat. And afterward, see if you still feel the same way about that person.

My point is that personal relationships are easy to form, and they matter. There are fewer people in Congress than in many high school graduating classes, and first we need to create opportunities for them to get to know each other as fellow human beings. While foreign travel may serve a useful purpose in that regard, one need not go to rural India or sub-Saharan Africa to cross the party barrier and get to know one's colleagues. This may sound like arranging a high school social, but in fact the hyperpartisan dysfunction in Congress makes it essential that its members adopt ways to make a fundamental change in the mindset they bring to Washington. One freshman member interviewed in late 2010 told a reporter that he saw his identity as that of a Republican whose job it was to block Democrats from achieving their goals. He walked into the House of Representatives wearing a flaming red "R" and on the lookout for any poor "D," to whose defeat he was committed.

When he was a member of Congress, Republican Ray LaHood of Illinois (now President Barack Obama's secretary of transportation) worked with Representative David Skaggs of Colorado to arrange bipartisan retreats that would enable members and their families to come together away from Washington. LaHood, who had previously been the chief of staff to House Republican Leader Bob Michel, and Skaggs, a Democrat, understood that it is hard to demonize somebody you actually know and with whom you've spent some time. If you know the names of a colleague's children and favorite sports teams, and have a sense of who that individual is as a human being, you are much more likely to be able to sit down together and try to determine whether there are possible areas of agreement between your divergent political viewpoints. Neither LaHood nor Skaggs is still in Congress, but the challenge remains. Each year the Speaker of the House and the minority leader, as the leaders of their respective parties, should cohost a bipartisan retreat and make a serious effort to persuade their members to participate. The party leaders in the Senate should do the same.

The current congressional calendar calls for most legislative work to be done on Tuesdays, Wednesdays, and Thursdays, with legislators heading to Reagan Airport on Thursday evening and returning to Washington Monday evening or early Tuesday morning. Norman Ornstein of the American Enterprise Institute and other campaigners for a more bipartisan approach to governing have frequently suggested keeping members of Congress in session three full weeks every month, including the occasional Saturday, with one week available each month for meeting with constituents back in one's home state. House Republicans favored a full workweek in Washington back in the 1980s, when I was chair of the party's policy committee, but the idea has met predictable resistance. The current system has advantages—members of Congress can spend much more time meeting with constituents—but the price is high: few members get to know each other, and in the absence of friendship or even cordial collegiality, the willingness to cooperate is less and the urge to demonize is greater. Personal relationships are critical for enabling any group to function, but the current operating system makes building such relationships extremely difficult. Ornstein has gone so far as to propose that the government create apartment complexes where members could live during their time in office, with common dining areas. That idea is unlikely to generate much support—members of Congress are as entitled as any other citizen to choose where they want to live and send their children to school—but the fact that Ornstein, one of the Congress's most astute observers, would toy with the idea is an indication of how damaging it is to have members of Congress know each other not as people but primarily as wearers of the letter D or R.

I direct the Aspen Institute's Rodel leadership program for elected officials. The program brings in mayors and city council leaders, lieutenant governors, state treasurers, attorneys general, and state house and senate leaders for three weekend sessions and one week of foreign travel, and each fellowship class is evenly divided between Republicans and Democrats. But there is one element of the program that is central to our success in breaking down party divisions. On the opening night of the first seminar of each class, we take a couple of hours, sometimes more, to have all of the members of the class introduce themselves as people: their families, where they're from, why they entered politics, what is important to them. We begin not by learning Aristotle but by learning about each other. It is a practice desperately needed in Congress.

No Labels, which is working to push Congress to act in a more bipartisan way, has proposed monthly bipartisan gatherings in the Old Senate Chamber in the Capitol, at which House and Senate members could informally discuss the upcoming legislative calendar and the most urgent problems facing the country, with no cameras or reporters or interest group representatives present. When Jim Wright, as Speaker, attempted to arrange private meetings between leaders from both sides of the aisle, we met once, and never again, but a commitment by the leaders of both parties in both the House and Senate to sponsor the sessions on a regular basis could help break down the warfare that pervades both chambers. Many reformers believe everything the Congress does should be done in the light of day, and there is certainly a case to be made for as much transparency as possible. But any simplistic reform invites unintended and unwelcome consequences. Transparency is essential to keeping government accountable, but so is the ability of public leaders to privately explore possible areas of agreement without facing accusations of selling out the unreasonable expectations of hard-line partisans.

The House and Senate should also encourage members to participate in the unofficial organizations that have their basis in concerns other than party and bring together Republicans and Democrats whose commonalities at least temporarily transcend their club memberships. The House Rust Belt Caucus, for example, brings together legislators from the upper Midwest states that have been struggling economically for decades. Other informal and bipartisan caucuses unite representatives from farm states, or those who have an interest in America's trade balance or in protecting intellectual property. The Aspen Institute's Congressional Program, now directed by former congressman and Cabinet secretary Dan Glickman, hosts a weekly breakfast meeting at which members of both the House and Senate, from both parties, meet to hear presentations from experts on a variety of public issues. Even the House gym, the least partisan place in Washington, has members who meet regularly and leaders who oversee the gym's management. All of us who work out there do so in gym shorts and T-shirts, and because party membership has nothing to do with where one's locker is located or how large it is, members are more inclined to talk to each other civilly about vacations, family, football, and other elements of everyday life. When George H. W. Bush was president, he was authorized to use the House gym by virtue of his two terms in Congress; one could often find the Republican president on the handball court with Democratic friends with whom he had forged long-standing relationships on the court and on the treadmills. When Hillary Clinton was a member of the Senate, she frequently attended prayer breakfasts, where she soon became friends with Sam Brownback, a conservative Republican. The development of such personal relationships is important if the Congress is to function effectively, and it is the responsibility of congressional leaders to actively promote such informal opportunities to break down the partisan barriers that have made political compromise so difficult and have engendered so much political nastiness.

Political observers have often found it strange that in an electorate that holds the Congress in shockingly low esteem (at times during 2011 congressional approval dropped below 10 percent), an amazingly large number of voters have until recently remained positive about their own senators and representatives. One reason for this seeming disconnect is that voters actually know their own members of Congress and judge them not only on the performance of the institution but by their individual qualities. Sometimes one meets a member of Congress from another part of the country, perhaps from a different political party, and is surprised to find that the person is actually pleasant, appears to have the country's best interests at heart, and is intelligent. This is an important discovery. Members of Congress, regardless of party identification or political philosophy, generally love their country, want it to do well, and have the education, experience, and intelligence to work in the national interest. If only they could come together to do so.

Party leaders will always try to bring their members in line behind the party's agenda, but the more our senators and representatives are able to think of themselves as part of the same team—the American team—rather than as troops in enemy camps, the sooner we will be able to find solutions to the difficult problems that challenge any major modern nation.

TEN

The Partisan Presidency

Step Nine: Eliminate One-Party White House Strategy Sessions

For most of this book I have concentrated on the legislative branch of government, because it is a collective institution in which groups of people have divided themselves into rival camps. The presidency, on the other hand, is singular: there are thousands of men and women in the executive branch, but only one Chief Executive. While a president may sometimes find himself of two minds about a goal or an action, he can hardly be described as at war with himself. Yet presidents are every bit as much to blame for the excessive partisanship of our time. Especially as elections near, the president often pushes legislation designed to satisfy his party's political base, both to boost his chances for reelection and to bolster his party's prospects.

Just like members of Congress, presidents will always pursue their own agendas, as they should. But whether a president has been elected in a romp or a squeaker, most decisions are not finally his to make. As columnist Ezra Klein put it in the *Washington Post*, "It is simply the reality of the American presidency. Congress can write legislation and pass it over the president's veto. The President cannot write legislation nor pass it without congressional assent. The President comes after the Congress in the Constitution and is indisputably less powerful. Yet we understand American politics primarily through the office of the President and attribute, say, things that happened between 1933 to 1945 to FDR, or from 1980 to 1988 to Ronald Reagan."[1] Both the presidency's importance in the public mind and presidents' need of the Congress if they are to have any chance of seeing their proposals adopted provide ample reasons for the White House to attempt to reduce the level of partisan warfare on Capitol Hill, especially if at least one house is controlled by the opposition party. And there are ways to do that.

As a member of the House Republican leadership during the Reagan and George H. W. Bush presidencies, I met with the president at least once a week in the Cabinet room at the White House. The usual gathering included the president, the vice president, key members of the Cabinet, and the four senior Republican leaders in the House and Senate. At other times I and others met with senior administration officials in the Roosevelt Room or, on difficult foreign policy issues, in the basement situation room. Who was not in those meetings? Even though Democrats then had large majorities in the House and, most of the time, in the Senate, these meetings were for Republicans only; members of the Democratic leadership were rarely included, even though Reagan and Democratic Speaker Tip O'Neill, two genial, joke-swapping Irishmen, had a comfortable informal relationship.

Presidents may have less formal authority than is generally believed, and less than the presidents of many other countries, but there is an aura to the presidency—the office once occupied by George Washington, Thomas Jefferson, Abraham Lincoln, and Franklin Roosevelt— that makes a call from the president, a flight on Air Force One, or a visit to the White House something that even the most powerful member of Congress will drop into every conversation for months. All but the most senior legislators will find a call from a Cabinet member or a member of the president's staff noteworthy. Given that special magic, whoever occupies the White House has a great ability to transcend the partisan division in Congress. Supporters of a president's agenda often argue, without much basis, that the president's policies deserve deference because he is the only public official in America who is elected by citizens of all fifty states. That unique credential does not translate into monarchical authority, but a president does nonetheless have a moral obligation to step outside the narrow Republican-Democrat, liberal-conservative, urban-rural, producer-consumer divisions that occupy other officials. The president is the head of one branch of the federal government, not a designated party leader, and he, more than any other public official, has the stature to ignore the constraints of partisanship.

One way to start that process is by discontinuing the practice of presidents meeting primarily with members of their own political party. Going to the White House for a meeting with the president is never, no matter how often you've done it, a ho-hum affair, and the simple act of making such an event an occasion for an honest conversation among the leaders of the executive and legislative branches of government, from both parties, might change the tenor of those conversations and open the door to political solutions that would benefit the entire nation. Note that I did not say it will change things. For such a bold, transcendent step to be effective, the president will have to remember that while he may be the host, he is not the regal personage many presidents have supposed themselves to be; the Congress is completely independent of the presidency and completely its equal, and though the powers of the legislature are more diffuse, they are every bit as real. This cannot be an occasion for a president to lecture members of Congress (they are neither his employees nor his students); it must be one in which the president chairs a discussion among peers.

That only a president can pull off such a feat is so evident as to impose an obligation on the president to make it happen. I've previously noted that when Jim Wright became the Speaker of the House, he often acted in a very partisan way, especially in increasing the number of House bills sent to the floor under a rule that forbade members to offer amendments. But Wright also made attempts to forge greater bipartisanship in the institution. On one occasion, he tried to get both parties to sign off on a nationwide polling service to give the same survey data to all House members (as the Republican representative to the discussions, I decided against our participation on the grounds that such a new taxpayer-funded poll would be an unnecessary expense given the abundance of similar surveys available, but the motive behind Wright's proposal was probably a good one). On another occasion—which in hindsight seems almost surreal—Wright, in one of his first days as Speaker, invited the senior leadership of both parties to a meeting in a small Ways and Means Committee room across from the Members' Dining Room on the first floor of the Capitol. The idea was to have the four top Republican leaders and their Democratic counterparts begin a series of joint conversations to forge an agreement on the outlines of the year's schedule. To signify the hope behind the gesture, Wright presented each of us (all men, as it happened) with blue neckties depicting red donkeys and elephants dancing together. It was the first and only such meeting; I still have the necktie as the only remaining indication that such a meeting had ever taken place.

Given the partisanship that has seeped into every corner of the Congress, and the incentives that inevitably pit one party against the other, the need for presidential leadership is obvious. One place to start is with the president's legislative liaison. Political junkies can often name most of a president's top staff members—press secretaries and chiefs of staff, security advisers, and economic advisers—but few can name even one member of the team the president deploys each day to engage with his allies and opponents on Capitol Hill. While most would agree that the success of Ronald Reagan's presidency had more to do with his personal charm than with the makeup of his White House staff, it owed much to the effective liaison operation he maintained with representatives and senators on both sides of the aisle, whether in leadership positions or not. By contrast, Jimmy Carter's presidency, which was much less successful, was plagued by a largely inept outreach to Congress. Acting on behalf of the president, the liaison team has enormous potential to help find the common interests that can bridge the ever-deeper partisan chasm that divides members of Congress from each other and the Congress from the people.

Presidents run as the nominees of their parties and have a shared affinity with their fellow partisans, but once elected they must step outside the partisan box and energetically don the role of national leader. I have said many times that the president is not the "head of government"—the United States does not have a head of government, and he is only "head" of one of three separate and equal branches—but he is nonetheless the head of state: the nation's principal spokesman and the one person with the aura and constituency to transcend party divisions. To a large extent, Dwight Eisenhower, who came to the presidency as a war hero and university president rather than as a traditional political figure, embodied a bigger-than-party persona (Democrats had also tried to persuade him to run on their ticket), but no other president of the past century has filled the same sort of national role. It is something America badly needs. Because the lawmaking power, the taxing power, the spending power, and the war power are all in the Congress, a president's greatest contribution can be to lay out his own views as to what should be done and then work to bring members of Congress together—not to support his policies but to find areas of common ground, to be the "uniter" that President George W. Bush promised to be but wasn't, and the "above partisanship" president that Barack Obama promised to be but hasn't been.

Presidents often call upon the members of Congress to come together, but generally what they mean is that members should come together in support of the president's agenda. From the perspective of the White House, directives flow in one direction, from the principal to the students. But to the frustration of the "principal," that is not how our constitutional system was designed. Presidents who hold back information (as they tend to do when submitting names to the Senate for confirmation to executive branch appointments, sharing information about the management of federal programs, or divulging military and foreign policy initiatives) merely pour fuel on the fires of contention. The branches are separate and independent, but that does not mean they cannot cooperate. For members of Congress, keeping a check on the president's administration of the government should not require micromanagement or hostility; for the White House, protecting the independence of the presidency should not require paternalism, dismissiveness, or executive arrogance. The branches are separate, but they are separate branches of the same tree. Over the years, presidents have been every bit as culpable as the Congress in creating the incivility and partisan combativeness that make compromise and progress increasingly difficult. Now they must take a leadership role in bridging the partisan divide.

ELEVEN

Declarations of Independence

Step Ten: Sign No Pledges, Stand Up to Bullies

The title of this chapter is borrowed from Part 4 of John Avlon's book *Independent Nation*, in which he points to American political leaders, from Margaret Chase Smith to Rudy Giuliani, whom he considers exemplars of great courage in the face of intense political pressure.[1] John F. Kennedy did the same thing in his Pulitzer Prize–winning book, *Profiles in Courage*, a chronicle of United States senators who stood up to the demands of their constituents when they believed the good of the nation required it.[2] Just as Kennedy sought examples of political courage, the Greek philosopher Diogenes reportedly spent his days searching for an honest man. If we wish to emulate Kennedy and Diogenes in searching for exemplars of courage and honesty, we might begin by demanding of our lawmakers that they courageously and honestly embrace the responsibilities of thoughtfulness, reflection, and honest appraisal that their oaths promise and self-government requires.

Members of Congress, when they are sworn in, take a very specific oath, which states in part: "I will support and defend the Constitution of the United States against all enemies, foreign and domestic. . . . I take this obligation freely, without any reservation or purpose of evasion, and . . . I will well and faithfully discharge the duties of the office on which I am about to enter. So help me God."

In taking this oath, one acknowledges that one is assuming not only an honor but a great obligation, and that it is undertaken freely and without reservation (that is, not conditionally and not subject to other commitments). The obligation is enormous—to decide what to tax and how much to tax it, to pay the nation's debts, to provide for the nation's general welfare, to regulate both domestic and international trade, to declare (or not declare) war, to govern and regulate the armed forces (no, that's not a presidential prerogative), and to govern the militias (national guard) when they are called to federal service. And to make all the laws necessary to carry into execution all of the powers vested in any part of the federal government.

That's an awesome responsibility.

And yet, every two years, hundreds of members of Congress raise their hands in the Senate and the House of Representatives and take that oath while fully aware that they have already violated it, having committed their loyalty to others, and to other agendas. Before a single word of testimony has been heard, before a bill has even been drafted and made available for perusal, before any facts have been gathered and the arguments evaluated, their decisions have already been made. On the one hand, there is the sworn oath to faithfully assume the great duties of a member of Congress "without any reservation," and on the other hand, a pledge of fealty to interest groups.

The private group Americans for Tax Reform, led by conservative activist Grover Norquist, demands a commitment by all candidates for Congress that if they are elected they will not support any attempt to raise federal taxes. Amazingly, all over the country, hundreds of candidates have agreed to that constraint without knowing whether at some point the United States might find itself in a desperate war for survival against state-sponsored terrorism, or with some of its major cities devastated by flood or fire, or with millions of Americans cut down by an epidemic. By November 2010, according to the Washington newspaper *The Hill*, a number of Republican members of Congress, some claiming they had agreed to the pledge years earlier, intending it be binding only for the following Congress, began to disavow the no-new-taxes pledge.[3] Norquist's organization claimed that 238 House members—a clear majority—had agreed to be bound with no time limit, and threatened to campaign against them if they broke their word. His tax pledge, *New York Times* columnist David Brooks has written, "isn't really about public policy; it's a chastity belt Republican politicians wear to show that they haven't been defiled by the Washington culture."[4]

In Iowa in 2011, Republican candidates for president were pressed to take a pledge to oppose gay marriage and to resist the imposition of shari'a law. These imperatives led to the spectacle of men and women who would have us consider them capable of serving as president—a position in which they might find themselves forced to stand up to mighty foreign powers with arsenals capable of destroying cities—meekly caving in to the demands of citizens whose greatest threat is that they might vote for somebody else. Former Minnesota Governor Tim Pawlenty, briefly a candidate for president, bravely refused to sign such a pledge . . . until he timidly retreated and added his signature in an attempt to fend off the threatened retaliation. Other groups have demanded that candidates make a pledge not to pay the nation's debts (a specific constitutional obligation) until after the Congress has enacted a balanced budget amendment. The National Women's Law Center insists that candidates sign a pledge to support pay equity legislation.

Let us accept that all of those positions are legitimate and that the men and women who advocate them are well-intentioned. But if the pledges mean anything, once a candidate for office signs one he or she surrenders the freedom of action—the oath to act without reservation—that we have a right to expect from the men and women we elect to positions of national leadership. (Ironically, the very insistence that a candidate put a commitment in writing suggests that we don't believe he or she can be trusted, in which case only a fool would vote for such a person.)

The worst part of having signed such a pledge is that an honest candidate will feel a moral obligation not to violate the commitment, thus shutting down the possibility of compromise. Here's an example that should send chills down the spine of any thoughtful person. Republicans have generally argued that federal spending has gotten out of control; yes, taxes are too high, they say, but the taxes are high because we have spent too much. Therefore, cutting back on the size and cost of government has been one of the stated goals of the Republican Party for decades. During the 2011 negotiations over raising the debt ceiling, one proposal would have included a promise to cut eight dollars of federal spending for every dollar of new tax revenues, seemingly a unique opportunity to make almost unimaginable progress toward the goal of shrinking government. Even starting with the premise that the American people are not undertaxed, even granted that every new dollar taken in taxes is an impediment to economic growth, a significant slashing of federal expenditures would have seemed like a good trade-off and, for Republicans, a signal victory—spending cuts now plus reduced taxes in the future. One could argue, as many did, that the deal was "not good enough"; this is a valid point of view. But what was not valid, what violated the very essence of the congressional oath of office and the constitutional obligations each member of Congress had assumed, was the unwillingness to seriously consider the various alternatives because of pledges to an outside organization that precluded the diligence we should expect from our elected leaders. The ability to compromise—the central requirement for the effective governance of a large and diverse nation—was destroyed, and we were thrown into a continuing crisis in which the world watched to see whether the United States would pay its debts.

The oath of office requires loyalty to the Constitution—not to the president, to a political party, or to any outside organization demanding fealty. No man or woman should enter Congress with divided loyalties. It is time for every candidate to refuse to sign any pledge, or take any oath, other than to "fully discharge the duties upon which they are about to enter. So help me God."

PART IV

A New Politics

TWELVE

Beyond Partisanship

Many of the bloggers and anonymous online posters who vent their frustrations at Congress's performance routinely engage in hyperbole or outright falsehood about almost every aspect of congressional service (awesome pensions payable after a single term of service, health care coverage and retirement packages unavailable to "the rest of us," etc.). One of the more common canards is that members of Congress are not well enough educated, or experienced, for the jobs they hold. At a 2011 conference of humanities scholars I attended as a panelist, one speaker asserted without challenge that the most common highest level of educational attainment for members of Congress was a high school degree. First we have to determine how true this claim is, and if it's not, what accounts for the dysfunction that even many members of Congress have publicly noted?

Do the facts indicate that the fault lies with the backgrounds of the people we elect? In the 111th Congress (2009–10), two hundred fifteen members of Congress had law degrees, including five with advanced law degrees; ninety-nine had master's degrees, and twenty-three had PhDs. Five had been Rhodes Scholars, three had been Fulbright Scholars. Five were engineers and six were scientists. Thirteen had been members of the White House staff or White House Fellows; thirty-eight had been mayors; two had served in president's cabinets; three had been state supreme court justices. The Congress included a former ambassador, a former federal judge, an admiral who had commanded a carrier battle group, and an astronaut. By every measure of attainment, including education, members of Congress represent the best among us. So what's missing?

Waist-deep in the mire of political battle, dealing with hundreds of proposals in every congressional session, and under constant pressure to remain loyal to party (and, if he's a member of the same party, the president) and to follow Sir Joseph's maxim of "never thinking for myself at all," any member of Congress, no matter how well prepared, would find it hard to rise above the conflict in order to be able to put things in perspective, to remember the lessons absorbed over time. As the saying goes, "It's hard to remember you set out to drain the swamp when you're up to your neck in alligators" (yes, I cleaned it up). But without the ability to put the day's issues in context or to reflect on the lessons of history, decisions become simply a matter of having "a point of view" without careful analysis of whether it's a good point of view. Marty Linsky, a Harvard professor who teaches public leadership, often talks of the need for elected officials to "get off the dance floor and climb up to the balcony," where they can get a clearer picture of whatever situation demands attention.

A successful democracy is largely dependent on shared values and a commitment to civil discourse. A nation that is allergic to nuance and complexity can offer little guidance to its elected officials; a nation that cannot tolerate ambiguity or weigh evidence cannot easily be brought together in a common understanding of the community's problems, much less in a reasoned conversation about proposals to address those problems. (This is why the decline in educational standards and the disappearance of classroom instruction in civics and critical thinking are so devastating to our attempts at self-government.)

It has long been assumed that the conflicts within the House and Senate are so seemingly unbridgeable because they rest on the embrace of divergent values. But if Representative A and Representative B simply disagree on the "right" course of action—the one responsive to the highest values—compromise is still possible because there are often ways to accommodate those differences. If, for example, A places the highest premium on the protection of individual choice (the "liberty" imperative) and B values collective responsibility (the "social" obligation), solutions can be found that address communal problems using incentives rather than coercion, and creating minimal interference with freedom of choice. Another, less attractive, assumption has been at play as well. Liberals and Democrats sometimes tend to believe that conservatives and Republicans are either mean-spirited or—a shoulder shrug and an eye roll here—not very smart. Republicans and conservatives have the same view of Democrats and liberals: they just don't get it, and those who do get it don't seem to care very much about the rights of the housewife/shop owner/investor. But here, too, compromise seems attainable if the opposing sides are able to marshal enough voices in town meetings and visits to congressional offices to force attention to the impacts of A's or B's proposals.

George Mason University economics professor Daniel B. Klein put his finger on one of the most difficult obstacles in the way of creating a Congress that is more amenable to cooperation and compromise.[1] His observation came after he discovered a bias that prompted him to retract a study he had done a year earlier. Klein said that the study, which he conducted with Zeljka Buturovic, a public opinion researcher with a doctorate in psychology, found that respondents who had identified themselves as liberals or progressives "did much worse than conservatives and libertarians" when it came to "real-world understanding of basic economic principles." Klein (who describes himself as libertarian) subsequently published a summation of their findings in the *Wall Street Journal*, arguing that their research demonstrated that, as he later summarized it, "the American left was unenlightened, by and large, as to economic matters." That article was headlined "Are You Smarter Than a Fifth Grader," thus suggesting that liberals are not. However, Klein and Buturovic subsequently did a follow-up study that showed that their original findings had been wrong; if the survey were done differently, they found, "under the right circumstances, conservatives and libertarians were as likely as anyone on the left to give wrong answers to economic questions."

Superficially, this would seem to be a reassuring discovery: rather than a case of dummies battling geniuses, it's simply a matter of conflicting views held by equally well-intentioned and intelligent competitors. But in fact the implications of what Klein and Buturovic found are quite disturbing, especially if one hopes for a Congress more inclined toward cooperation. "The proper inference from our work," Klein wrote in the *Atlantic*, "is not that one group is more enlightened or less. It's that 'myside bias'—the tendency to judge a statement according to how conveniently it fits with one's settled position—is pervasive among all of America's political groups." In other words, given a set of possible conclusions, politicians, like the rest of us, will choose not the one that comports with dispassionate analysis but the one that fits their own preconceptions. This was a common occurrence during the Cold War, with one group of Americans arguing that deploying space-based defensive missiles would increase our security, and others arguing that such a provocative deployment would increase the chances of war. Does government spending hurt or harm economic growth? Do relaxed college admissions requirements help or hurt disadvantaged students? Everybody reading these questions will "know" the right answers, but the answers each of us gives will likely be the ones that fit our preconceptions about the proper role of government, the roles of nature and nurture, and the relative benefits of "tough love" and "comforting" love. We and our elected officials are operating from different ideas as to what the facts are. And while we may be willing to find common ground, we will do so within the facts we think we know. "Myside bias"—choosing the "fact" that validates your side's position—makes compromise almost inconceivable. If I "know" you are wrong, I can only try to stop you.

Nobody made the case for government as a cooperative enterprise more compellingly than Benjamin Franklin. Delegates to the Constitutional Convention were of many minds, and debate was robust. Franklin did not agree with all elements of the Constitution that finally emerged from the long debates and many compromises. But on the last day of the convention, September 17, 1787—the date we now celebrate as Constitution Day—Franklin, who was old and weak, wrote out an impassioned plea and gave it to his fellow Pennsylvania delegate, James Wilson, to read. Franklin readily admitted that there were parts of the Constitution "which I do not at present approve" but, he added, "I am not sure I shall never approve them. For having lived long, I have experienced many instances of being obliged by better information, or fuller consideration, to change opinions even on important subjects, which I once thought right, but found to be otherwise. It is therefore that the older I grow, the more apt I am to doubt my own judgment, and to pay more respect to the judgment of others." Franklin closed his remarks with an appeal to his fellow delegates to join him in approving the Constitution that guides us today. "On the whole, sir," he wrote, "I cannot help expressing a wish that every member of the Convention who may still have objections to it would, with me, on this occasion, doubt a little of his own infallibility, and to make manifest our unanimity, put his name to the instrument."

On October 2, 2011, retired Supreme Court Justice David Souter and I participated in a symposium, titled American Institutions and a Civil Society, at the induction meeting of the American Academy of Arts and Sciences. Calling compromise the "required practice" in our constitutional system, Souter noted that historian Jack Rakove had described compromise as the "necessary condition" that allowed the Founders to resolve the important differences that confronted them in Philadelphia.[2] Constitutional lawyers, Souter said, "find it disquieting when the America polity seems to speak most loudly in terms of anti-compromise: that is, in terms of a rigid absolutism of principle on the part of one speaker or another, or indeed, on the part of one major political party or another." He issued a dire warning: "How long can we expect the American people to support a Constitution that is demonstrably inconsistent with the daily practice of politics in American life?"

This problem becomes even more intractable in the context of a Congress divided between rival teams, each operating from its own "facts" and each in a position to come down hard on any teammate who thinks for himself and begins to question the accepted orthodoxy. Eric Hoffer, in *The True Believer*, noted the penchant of individuals to seek to belong to something larger than themselves, something transcendent, a cause to which they can devote themselves and in which they can place their faith.[3] Writing in the *New York Times Magazine* in 1971, Hoffer observed that both absolute power and absolute faith demand "absolute obedience . . . simple solutions . . . the viewing of compromise as surrender."[4] When "true believers" are able to dominate a political party, for example through closed candidate selection processes, and can demand allegiance to their dogma, political rigidity ensues. When party leaders are given the additional authority to punish unfaithfulness, the compromise necessary for a functioning democracy disappears.

Are there ways, then, even given the current party system, to reduce partisanship and encourage more independent thinking? Marcel Proust wrote that "the real voyage of discovery consists not in seeking new landscapes, but in having new eyes." If members of Congress come to their tasks with eyes fixed firmly on their responsibilities as part of a political machine, we can expect no more from them than what we have been getting. But if we open their eyes to the bigger entity to which they owe loyalty, we can change their behavior. Two of the nation's premier scholars, University of Pennsylvania President Amy Gutmann and Harvard Professor Dennis Thompson, addressed the problem in a November 2011 op-ed in the *New York Times*. Noting that "there is no external escape from an environment that rewards those who stand tenaciously on their principles and demonize their opponents," Gutmann and Thompson put it very bluntly: "Members of Congress need to change their minds about compromise, or voters will need to change the members of Congress."[5]

Earlier we considered the negative impact on the government's ability to function when political battles prevent the filling of federal judgeships and other important positions. William Galston, a scholar at the Brookings Institution, has suggested at least one way of looking at the partisan wars through "new eyes." The Constitution provides for only one federal court—the Supreme Court—with the nominating power reserved exclusively to the president. Even in that instance, however, the president's authority extends only to putting forth the name of a nominee: actually placing somebody on the Supreme Court requires action by the Senate. All other federal courts have been established not by the Constitution but by acts of Congress, which therefore leaves to the Congress the ability to determine how those additional judges are to be selected. Currently, nominations for all federal judgeships are also made by the president, but because judicial appointments often lead to partisan battles, often without regard to whether or not the presidential nominee is actually qualified by experience or temperament, Galston has proposed largely removing the judicial confirmation process from the political arena. Bipartisan commissions would provide the White House with lists of possible nominees from which the president would make his selection, with the nominee then sent to the Senate for consideration under a "fast-track" procedure that would ensure rapid consideration. The Aspen Institute has moved in a similar direction, establishing a bipartisan task force (I'm a member) to recommend ways of speeding the confirmation process for key executive branch appointments, under procedures that would guarantee sufficient time for proper vetting of nominees but remove many of the expensive and unnecessary hurdles that many nominees now must survive even to reach the point of a Senate vote. Such a procedure would not only ensure that important government positions were filled but also remove such appointments from the list of issues over which the parties battle for public approval.

Here's another way to improve the workings of Congress. Years ago, I was invited to speak on a panel that included some of the most senior members of the House of Representatives, representing both political parties. The panelists held divergent views on most important political issues of the day, but there was one issue on which almost all were in agreement: the belief that the House had made a serious error in establishing, for the first time, a separate budget committee. Until 1974, when the committee was established under the chairmanship of Connecticut Congressman Robert Giaimo, the budgeting process was relatively simple. As each new Congress unfolded, various committees determined what federal programs to create, expand, close down, or reduce. The Ways and Means Committee, which is charged with establishing revenue policy and tax rates, produced its plan. The various appropriations (spending) sub-committees acted on the recommendations of the authorizing committees, determining how much to actually spend on each recommended program. Then, at the end of the process, the various pieces were brought together to create a final package. The Senate followed a similar procedure, and as is required with all legislation, the House and Senate versions were reconciled with each other in a conference committee that worked out the differences and presented both houses with a final version for approval. Most of the time this reconciliation process worked well. The Budget Committee, however, threw a wrench into the works.

As a member of both the Appropriations Committee and the Budget Committee, I watched the entire process get bogged down. Members were forced to wait for the Budget Committee to finish its work, with its own separate process of hearings and votes, before they could learn what the overall budget would allow each committee to spend. The budget "instructs" the committees but has no force of law, just as the budget submitted each year by the president—a task assigned to the president by the Congress—has no force in law and has at times been completely ignored. But this budget, unnecessary and toothless, brings the resolution of everything else to a standstill. And it greatly sharpens the partisan nastiness that now pervades the institution. Although the partisan conflict is played out in the authorizing and appropriating committees and subcommittees too, the fact that they are narrowly constructed—to deal with transportation issues, for example, or federal parklands—tends to make the discussions, and the debates, fact-based, and the differences more regional than philosophical. This is obviously not always the case; some areas of the law (banking regulation, for example) still bring out partisan differences, but it is the Budget Committee, charged with providing an overall blueprint for government priorities, where the lines are most starkly drawn and the passions most vigorously stirred. Unnecessarily beginning the lawmaking process with a largely partisan battle sets the stage for an unabated conflict that poisons subsequent committee work.

In October 2011, as a special budget "supercommittee"—made up of House and Senate members of both parties—ground on without progress, Senators Ben Cardin, a Maryland Democrat, and Kelly Ayotte, a first-term New Hampshire Republican, grumped that if the committee could not find agreement, even under the pressure of unsustainable budget deficits, Congress should just shut down altogether. Former Congressman Lee Hamilton, now director of the Center on Congress at Indiana University, told the *Washington Post* that when people say Congress is dysfunctional, "the budget process I think is Exhibit A."[6] Since the Budget Committee was created, the budget bill and all of the necessary appropriations bills have been passed on time only twice in almost forty years. The result has been a constant use of fallback "omnibus" bills, short-term stopgaps, and "continuing resolutions" that simply keep doing, for a while at least, what was done the year before, whether or not that addresses problems or allows sufficient oversight of federal agencies. Partisan warfare is exacerbated and Congress's ability to function is crippled. One does not often call for the elimination of a committee of which one has been a part, but the Budget Committee has proven to be an impediment to, not a facilitator of, compromise, conciliation, and bipartisan governance. It is past time to eliminate it.

There are also ways to encourage senators and representatives to think outside the confines of party identity. When new members of Congress are elected, they are offered several orientation sessions, none of which are required but each of which offers some beneficial instruction. The Library of Congress offers instruction in the nuances of legislative rules and behaviors as well as helpful tips about hiring and managing one's staff. I particularly remember one bit of advice that I never followed very well: your staff, we were told, is there to reduce your workload, not increase it. In other words, I was supposed to be giving them work to do; they weren't supposed to be giving me more work to do. That was fairly typical of the kinds of advice dispensed. After I left Congress and joined the faculty of Harvard's Kennedy School of Government, I sometimes took part in orientation seminars conducted by the school's Institute of Politics for newly elected House members. The institute's seminars offered helpful tips about which committee positions to seek, means of increasing one's influence in the House, and balancing time between Washington (where votes were to be cast) and one's home district (where votes were to be won). These sessions also attempted to bring these new members of Congress up to speed on the state of the economy and on major legislation that would come before them in the coming session of Congress (technically, each new Congress starts from scratch but in reality new members are entering in the middle of the movie). Organizations like the Heritage Foundation put on their own seminars, geared toward members of a particular philosophical orientation (conservatives, in this case) and painting the upcoming legislative session as seen through an ideological lens.

In the Fellowship seminars I run for the Aspen Institute, we take a different approach. Our first class, eight years ago, brought together elected officials of all political stripes—moderate Democrats like Arizona State Representative (and later Congresswoman) Gabby Giffords and liberal Democrats like Tom Perez, a local county council president in Maryland and later assistant U.S. attorney general; and conservative Republicans like Minnesota House majority leader (and now Congressman) Erik Paulsen and Maryland Lieutenant Governor (and later Republican National Chairman) Michael Steele. For four days at a time, three times over two years, we gathered together to talk about questions larger than the issues of the day. What, we asked, were the great values, the underlying principles, of a good society? What beliefs united us? What differences could be bridged? Our teachers were as varied as the Fellows themselves—Locke and Hobbes, Aristotle and Confucius. We focused not on the partisan battles but on the humanities: George Orwell, on duty in colonial India and wrestling with whether he was obligated to shoot a rogue elephant in order to demonstrate his leadership; Thucydides describing the governors of an island people weighing whether to submit or resist when threatened with the overwhelming force of Sparta—and whether to allow the people themselves a voice in the matter; Shelley reflecting on the fleeting nature of arrogance and power. These were matters to hone the questioning mind and attention to transcendent principles. Through it all, Gabby remained Gabby and Tom remained Tom; he's still a liberal and she's still a moderate. Mike and Erik are as Republican, and as conservative, as they were when they entered the program. But this disparate group of politicians with divergent and strongly held beliefs—of the kind that so often lead to animosity, distrust, and impermeable barriers to compromise or even civility—bonded together in a unique second family. When Gabby was shot years later as she was meeting with constituents, they came together to rally behind their wounded "sister." By bringing them together in a politics-free environment where they could mutually explore what unites them as Americans, we could make the walls crumble.

Undoubtedly, newly elected members of Congress will continue to seek out orientations that clue them in on how the constitutional system works and gives them an understanding of the issues they will confront. But it would be a good thing if House and Senate leaders would also schedule private, off-the-record opportunities for these newcomers to get to know each other over breakfast and Plato, with no position to defend, no partisan pledge to keep, and no labels to divide them.

THIRTEEN

The Way Forward

There are those who look at things the way they are, and ask why.
I dream of things that never were, and ask why not.
— ROBERT F. KENNEDY

I may not be able to look at things with the new eyes Proust recommends, but we should not assume that our federal government doesn't work. True, it's dysfunctional. It's a mess. It's a cafeteria food fight, kindergarten name-calling, a collection of whines, pouts, and threats to pick up one's marbles and go home. Trust in government, its institutions, and its elected leaders sinks ever lower, and even the rare moments of common satisfaction—over the elimination of the leader of al-Qaeda, for example—lift our opinions of government only slightly and briefly. But the government is working just as we've designed it to work, not for debate and deliberation but as a vehicle for partisan advantage-seeking.

It takes no genius to understand why things are the way they are: we have created a political system that rewards intransigence. Democracy requires divergence and honors dissent, but what we have today is not mere divergence and does not deserve the label "dissent"; it's a nasty battle for dominance, and it's often the dominance not of an idea or a great principle but of a private club that demands undeviating fealty.

Norman Ornstein, writing in the *Boston Review*, observed that when he first arrived in Washington from Minnesota in 1969, "there were two distinct seasons—a campaigning one and a governing one. Campaigns understandably used the metaphors of war. Governing, on the other hand, is an additive process, often requiring broad coalitions to craft significant public policy and to sell it to a public worried about short-term change. Norms reinforced this mindset: lawmakers would never campaign directly against their colleagues from other districts or states. . . . Campaign consultants and pollsters used to disappear after elections, but now they stick around as consultants, aides, and lobbyists, ever present."[1]

When I was first elected, I imagined that on taking the oath of office as a member of Congress I had crossed an invisible line from candidate and partisan to legislator. As Ornstein suggests, this line is no longer crossed. The campaign never ends, and the campaign mind-set—the free use of "the metaphors of war"—never abates. As a result, Ornstein wrote, "lawmakers from the other side of the aisle become almost radioactive. Working with them may give their side protection against attack on a wedge issue." (Since the time of Newt Gingrich's speakership, wedge issues have been a significant part of partisan efforts to use House debates not just to advance legislative policy but to drive a wedge between a congressperson of the other party and his or her constituents by forcing votes on amendments on which the views of constituents and party leaders are at odds.) Before the 1970s, votes on amendments were generally not recorded—House members voted by voice, by raising hands, or by walking down the center aisle to be counted. When small groups of members began to insist that votes on amendments, even those that reflected intentionally divisive wedge issues, be "on the record," Congress became more transparent and its members became more accountable, but at the cost of turning the House into a battle-ground for partisan advantage.

The advent of wedge issues wasn't alone in distorting the deliberative process. As Ornstein pointed out, members simultaneously "face mounting pressure to raise money as part of the team effort. . . . Any chance for serious debate or deliberation is brushed aside by the crushing imperative to raise funds." Between raising money for partisan warfare—party "dues" of up to $300,000 a year—and crafting "gotcha" votes to undercut members of the rival political team, time for thoughtful consideration of the legislative agenda became ever more scarce.

I do not object to political clubs; I belong to one. I don't object to these clubs making their preferences known in elections or in considering proposals that come before the Congress. But they cannot be allowed to control our politics. They cannot be allowed to limit our choices when we go to the polls to select the leaders who will shape the destiny of our country. We cannot allow them to deprive us of the right to be represented in the decision-making process by people who are familiar with our interests and concerns. We cannot allow them to gag more than a hundred million Americans by shutting their representatives out of effective participation in making the nation's laws.

But here's the thing: the leaders of those clubs will not voluntarily surrender the enormous power we have allowed them to accumulate. They can draw congressional districts to suit themselves, they can keep potential candidates off the ballot, and they can tell elected members of Congress that their views don't matter. In what way, exactly, does this resemble "democracy"? Do the holders of such powers ever willingly relinquish them? So egregious is the hold parties have over our election and governing systems that when they execute their closed primaries to choose their preferred candidates (and to keep others off the ballot), it is we, through our tax dollars, who pay for them to limit our choices. The two major political parties together received nearly $36 million from the federal government to stage their respective national conventions in 2012; the taxpayers' tab for "sponsoring" the party primaries in all fifty states costs many millions more. It is time to break free of the power these private clubs exercise over us and to tell them that they can no longer be in charge of drawing congressional district lines; that they can no longer keep potential candidates off the ballot just because they haven't been blessed by party activists; that they must allow divergent ideas to be debated and voted upon; and that they must pay for their own club events. We need that money for our schools and roads and health care expenses.

More than a century ago, fed up with the undemocratic backroom bossism that dominated American politics, the Progressives started a movement to return political power to the people. It was a grand and important idea, but over the years it has been transformed: now it's not a few insiders making the decisions, it's the zealots, the hyperpartisans, the true believers who accept no independent thought and punish those who would exercise it.

We won't fix the problem by sitting on our hands. Members of the Tea Party and Occupy movements began their protests against the current system by focusing on different concerns and using different tactics, but both accepted that real change requires activism. No Labels, the Bipartisan Policy Center, and Americans Elect have all come into being to try, through different means and emphases, to transcend the partisanship that has paralyzed government. In this book I've tried not only to highlight the problems and explain how we got to this point, but to suggest what changes are required—and, just as important, to show how those changes can be achieved.

In those states where voters are permitted to put issues directly on the ballot through the use of initiative petitions, concerned citizens will need to circulate petitions, gather signatures, publicize the issues, and wage statewide political battles, just as Californians did in 2010 when they took away much of the parties' power over the political system. In states that allow a referendum but not an initiative petition, citizens will need to confront state legislators and demand that they change election laws to permit open primaries and turn redistricting over to independent, nonpartisan commissions. If legislators resist, citizens must demand that they refer the issues to a public vote. Many legislators who are unwilling to vote for such far-reaching changes themselves will happily pass the buck.

Members of Congress are unlikely to be willing supporters of the changes I have proposed here. The majority party will not want to surrender the option of controlling the speakership, dominating committees, and denying a hearing to opponents. Members of the minority party undoubtedly chafe under the majority's tyranny, but they will want the same authority when they achieve a majority. Still, there remains one source of power that is greater than the party leaders: the voters themselves. As the Tea Party demonstrated, a forceful expression in a town meeting or congressperson's office is hard to dismiss. Every member of Congress should be put on notice that failure to advocate for these changes—requiring either a bipartisan or 60 percent vote for Speaker, removing the leadership's control over committee assignments, permitting votes on nontrivial alternative proposals, eliminating closed rules that preclude amendments—will earn retaliation from voters who are sick and tired of the partisanship that has so crippled government's ability to function. There is no more urgent task in American politics than to make fundamental change in how we govern ourselves.

Some will argue that other priorities are more urgent: creating jobs for the millions of our unemployed fellow citizens; making health care and education more affordable; improving the quality of our public schools; or any of a hundred other important matters on the public agenda, from national security to rebuilding our aging roads and highways. No one can dispute the enormity of those tasks or the importance of addressing them as soon as possible. But without fundamental political reform, the likelihood that those concerns will be addressed promptly or wisely is minimal at best. Each of them, and many other less critical issues, demand thoughtfulness, a fair assessment of the root problems, and an honest consideration of alternatives—none of which is likely in a system in which the battle for party dominance trumps every other consideration. So long as all the players in the decision-making process are focused on seeking out only those facts that support their predetermined positions, on ensuring that the presentation of other views is suppressed, and on eschewing compromise that might weaken one's hand in the next round of elections, schools will continue to be inadequate and costly, health care costs will threaten to rob one's entire lifetime savings, and jobs will continue to flow overseas. The system must be changed, and only you can bring that change about.

Many of the people who stood with the Occupy Wall Street movement believed that the individual citizen has been disempowered; that individually and collectively "the 99 percent" lack the ability to affect government decisions. In many ways, the disaffection they expressed mirrored that expressed from a different political perspective by the Tea Party activists who became engaged in the 2010 midterm elections that swung control of the House of Representatives to Republicans. While the Tea Party's impact on those elections has been greatly exaggerated, it is nonetheless true that what successes the Tea Party achieved came as a direct result of its members' ability to make themselves heard and to affect the outcome of several elections. The late Steve Jobs insisted on the Apple iPhone campaign that urged people to "think different." The correct usage would seem to be "think differently," but Jobs had a point: to think "different" is a much greater inversion of the normal process. If we want to change the current political system, we'll have to think different. And we will have to understand what is at stake. Yale law professor Akhil Amar calls the United States "the indispensable nation," the only nation in today's world that is capable of international leadership. As a result, he says, the decisions American citizens make affect people all over the world, and if those citizens are uninformed or disengaged, the whole world suffers. That may or may not be an overstatement, but it's clear that if American democracy fails, the reverberations will be felt far from our shores—this is not about us alone.

We have to reclaim our democracy, not from an invading army but from the parasitic destruction waged in the name of partisan interest. Because so many states allow citizens to take legislative action into their own hands through the initiative petition process, those who wish to eliminate closed partisan primaries or take away from political parties their current authority over legislative and congressional redistricting have means of doing so. The process for bringing those changes about is straightforward: once signatures have been gathered and their authenticity verified (states will vary as to specifics), the next step is to conduct a typical political campaign—raising money to get one's message out, finding volunteers to knock on voters' doors and send mailings supporting the initiative campaign, using websites and social media networks, and establishing a system to get voters to the polls. A referendum campaign, however, which must first pass proposals through the state legislatures before being put on a public ballot, or a campaign to change the way the Congress or the legislatures go about their business, is not about votes but about persuasion, whether gentle or confrontational.

Almost every member of Congress engages in frequent "town" or "neighborhood" meetings with constituents. While some limited these appearances after Arizona Congresswoman Gabrielle Giffords was shot, and others reverted to closed meetings with supporters in the wake of angry confrontations during the debates over health care reform, constituent meetings remain a staple of a legislator's life.

Not all constituents are voters, but all voters are constituents, and one ignores their message at the risk of becoming a "former" member of Congress. The problem has been that those who are truly bothered by a particular action, or inaction, by Congress dominate such meetings, putting the focus on the issue of the moment, not on the system that has failed to respond appropriately. The thoughtful but concerned rarely participate. Thus a member of Congress can stand before his or her constituents and brag of voting faithfully with the party line and not be challenged by those who find such partisan fealty outrageous. That must be changed: if your congressperson votes almost all the time with his or her party—as much as 90 percent of the time or more—it's fair to ask whether he or she is working for you or for a political club.

Pledge seekers have done great harm to the ability of legislators to draw upon their own knowledge to act in the national interest, and I do not support demanding a written commitment from any member of Congress, but they should nonetheless be challenged forthrightly about the need to change the speakership and the way committees function. They should be urged to abolish the two-lectern system in the House of Representatives and to open both cloakrooms and all computers on the House floor to members of both parties. They should be pushed to find opportunities to cosponsor bills or amendments with members of another party and to vote for proposals offered from across the aisle. And you should let them know—by mail, e-mail, and phone call, and in personal visits—that you are keeping tabs on whether they are actually doing so. Observe them as they use the lecterns or seat themselves in the chamber: changing the entire procedure in either the House or Senate is a difficult task, but insisting that your representatives act differently, and holding them accountable for doing so, is not difficult, and it should be done.

Because incentives work, it is up to you and your friends to change them: instead of responding to the loud voices demanding intransigence, legislators should instead be answering to the large numbers of you who are increasingly demanding bipartisanship and compromise. Both the House and Senate set their own rules at the beginning of every session of Congress. Rules governing filibusters can be changed: demand that your senator introduce the rules changes that will require filibustering senators to actually appear on the Senate floor to state their case. Press your representatives to offer rules changes to make the speakership and committee assignments more bipartisan. Launch a campaign to get your neighbors to vote in primaries and ask each of them to also demand these changes. Social media allow an unprecedented degree of community mobilization. Don't use Twitter or Facebook to tell your friends what you had for lunch—who really cares?—but use them to marshal a force to show up at town meetings, to visit a legislator's office, to demand bipartisan changes, and to vote in primaries for candidates who will agree to do so.

The beautiful thing about our governmental system is that, in the end, the power rests with us. We don't just determine whom we elect; we can also dictate how we elect them. In many states, legislators can submit issues to a vote of the people themselves. In addition, twenty-four states allow citizens to bypass the legislature altogether and put important questions—like changing the congressional redistricting process and eliminating closed party primaries—on the ballot.

The citizen initiative and the popular referendum—the most common forms of limited "direct democracy"—have been an important part of American governance for more than a century, dating back to 1898 when South Dakota amended its state constitution to permit voters to intervene in the lawmaking process whenever they believed their elected officials were not sufficiently responsive or were under the sway of special interests. Elizabeth Garrett, the provost at the University of Southern California, notes than 70 percent of all Americans now live in a state or city, or both, that allows them access to direct democracy. "The initiative process," she writes, "offers a way for voters to police their wayward legislative agents."[2] The Initiative and Referendum Institute reported in 2008 that from 1904, when the first statewide initiative appeared on Oregon's ballot, through 2007, 2,236 statewide initiatives had been presented to voters, and 908 (41 percent) had passed. There are additional benefits to the process: Garrett cites a 1996 study by Elisabeth Gerber of the Gerald R. Ford School of Public Policy, which concludes that "the possibility of the initiative process not only produces direct legislation that aligns with the preferences of the majority (or, more precisely, the median voter), but also induces legislators to move policy outcomes closer to the will of the majority." In fact, Garrett says, when legislators fully understand the popular will, they will act to ensure that a majority of voters are satisfied.

The initiative process, Garrett writes, is also being used to combat political polarization, "to attack anticompetitive electoral structures, and to realign institutions"—precisely what voters in her state of California did in 2010 when they used the initiative petition to eliminate closed party primaries and to take the redistricting power away from the state legislature and put it in the hands of a nonpartisan commission. Samuel Issacharoff has called this use of the initiative petition to change democratic institutions the "rebellion of the median voter."

The referendum process unfolds in a different way but can produce similar results. Whereas the initiative begins with citizen action aimed directly at other citizens—the drafting of a petition and the gathering of signatures to place an issue on the ballot—organizers of a referendum campaign begin by targeting state legislators, pressuring lawmakers either to make the desired changes themselves or to refer the issue directly to the voters. Either alternative requires citizens to go beyond mere anger and engage in a direct action to force change.

The many supportive letters, phone calls, and e-mails that followed the *Atlantic*'s publication of these suggestions in an article I wrote in 2011 inevitably ended with this cry: "But what can we do about it?"[3] Every American now alive has known only this system of government—two rival teams square off, draw congressional districts to their advantage, and tell us which candidates we must choose between. To imagine a different kind of system, with more choice, more honest representation, and more focus on the collective (and individual) good than on what's best for party insiders, seems beyond the imaginative capacity of a great many Americans. It will do no good for us simply to bemoan the inability of the federal government—our government—to serve our interests. We must also remind ourselves to regard each other simply as Americans—the bond we share—rather than as encampments of rival armies out to destroy each other.

I began this book by talking of you as a citizen, not a subject. As a citizen, take back your democracy. End partisan rule. Do it now.

Appendix: Citizen Initiative Information by State

The fastest way to bring about serious change—in expanding access to the ballot and creating congressional and state legislative districts that allow for the elections of true "representatives"—is by using the citizen initiative to force these changes in state law. The following table shows those states that allow initiatives, where to pick up the necessary petitions, where to file the petitions, and, by way of example, the deadlines for gathering signatures for the current election year and the number of signatures required. More information may be available from the National Association of Secretaries of State. Good luck, the ball is now in your court. Together we can make the changes our constitutional democracy requires.

TABLE 15.1: INITIATIVE PETITION INFORMATION BY STATE FOR THE 2012 GENERAL ELECTION

STATE	PETITION SOURCE	SIGNATURE REQUIREMENT	NUMBER OF SIGNATURES REQUIRED	DEADLINE FOR SUBMISSION
Arizona	Secretary of State 1700 W. Washington Street 7th Floor Phoenix, AZ 85007	10 percent of voters in the previous gubernatorial election	172,809	Four months before the general election
Arkansas	Secretary of State State Capitol, Room 256 Little Rock, AR 72201	8 percent of voters in the previous gubernatorial election, including 4 percent of voters in at least fifteen counties	62,507	Four months before the general election
California	Attorney General California Department of Justice P.O. Box 944255 Sacramento, CA 94224-2550	5 percent of voters in previous gubernatorial election	504,760	150 days after the secretary of state issues petitions, and at least 131 days before the general election
Colorado	Secretary of State 1700 Broadway Suite 200 Denver, CO 80290	5 percent of voters in previous secretary of state election	86,105	Six months after titles are set, and at least three months before the general election
Idaho	Secretary of State P.O. Box 83720 Boise ID 83720-0080	6 percent of the qualified electors in the previous general election	47,432	Four months before the general election
Missouri	Secretary of State Elections Division P.O. Box 1767 Jefferson City, MO 65102	5 percent of voters in each of two-thirds of the state's congressional districts	N/A	May 6, 2012

Appendix

State	Petition Source	Signature Requirement	Number of Signatures Required	Deadline for Submission
Montana	Secretary of State P.O. Box 202801 Helena, MT 59620-2801	5 percent of the votes cast in the previous gubernatorial election—signatures must come from at least 5 percent of voters in each of at least one-third of the legislature's House districts (34)	24,337	Sponsors to be notified of deadline by July 23, 2012
Nebraska	Secretary of State P.O. Box 94608 Lincoln, NE 68509-4608	7 percent of registered voters at the filing deadline—5 percent of voters in at least thirty-eight counties—must receive support from 35 percent of voters in the election	N/A until filing deadline	Four months before the general election
North Dakota	Secretary of State 600 E Boulevard Ave. Dept. 108 Bismarck, ND 58505-0500	2 percent of the statewide population	13,452	Ninety days before the general election
Oklahoma	Secretary of State 2300 N. Lincoln Boulevard Suite 101 Oklahoma City, OK 73105-4897	8 percent of voters in previous gubernatorial election	82,782	No deadline specified
Oregon	Secretary of State 255 Capitol Street NE Suite 501 Salem, OR 97310-1306	6 percent of voters in previous gubernatorial election	87,213	Four months before the general election

continued

TABLE 15.1 *continued*

STATE	PETITION SOURCE	SIGNATURE REQUIREMENT	NUMBER OF SIGNATURES REQUIRED	DEADLINE FOR SUBMISSION
South Dakota	Secretary of State Capitol Building 500 East Capitol Ave Pierre, SD 57501	5 percent of voters in previous gubernatorial election	15,855	November 1, 2011
Utah	Lieutenant Governor Utah State Capitol Suite 220 Salt Lake City, UT 84114	10 percent of votes cast in previous presidential election (from at least fifteen counties, representing at least 10 percent of the statewide votes for president)	96,234	316 days after the initiative petition is filed, or April 15, 2012 (whichever comes first)
Washington	Secretary of State Election Division P.O. Box 40229 Olympia, WA 98504	8 percent of voters in the previous gubernatorial election	241,153	Ten months before the general election—signatures must be filed four months before the general election

Notes

Preface

1. Mickey Edwards, "How to Turn Republicans and Democrats into Americans," *Atlantic*, July/August 2011.
2. Geoffrey Stone, "Induction Symposium: American Institutions and a Civil Society," *American Academy of Arts & Sciences Bulletin*, Winter 2012.
3. Mary Curtis, "Take Politics Off the Playground," *Root*, November 10, 2011.
4. Alan Abramowitz, *The Disappearing Center: Engaged Citizens, Polarization, and American Democracy* (New Haven: Yale University Press, 2010).
5. Peter Baker, "Hip, Hip—if Not Hooray—for a Standstill Nation," *New York Times*, June 18, 2011.

ONE
American Tribalism

1. Sean Wilentz, *The Rise of American Democracy: Jefferson to Lincoln* (New York: W. W. Norton, 2005).
2. Peter Shane, *Madison's Nightmare: How Executive Power Threatens American Democracy* (Chicago: University of Chicago Press, 2009).
3. Alan Abramowitz, *The Disappearing Center: Engaged Citizens, Polarization, and American Democracy* (New Haven: Yale University Press, 2010).

187

4. Francis Barry, *The Scandal of Reform: Grand Failures of New York's Political Crusaders and the Death of Nonpartisanship* (New Brunswick, NJ: Rutgers University Press, 2009).
5. David Brooks, "The Two Moons," *New York Times,* November 21, 2011.
6. Bill Bishop, *The Big Sort: Why the Clustering of Like-Minded America Is Tearing
Us Apart* (Boston: Houghton Mifflin Harcourt, 2008).
7. Susan Page, "USA Fumes over Politics," *USA Today,* April 2, 2010.
8. David Rogers, "For Many Swing Voters, Decision Turns on a Few Tough
Questions," *Wall Street Journal,* November 6, 2006.
9. Jeremy Jacobs, "Year of the Independent Voter," *Washington Independent, May
16, 2008.*
10. Rhodes Cook, "Voter Turnout and Congressional Change," Pew Research
Center Publications, November 1, 2006, http://pewresearch.org/pubs/83/
voter-turnout-and-congressional-change.
11. Richard Wolf, "Frustrated Voters Cut Ties with Democrats, Republicans,"
USA TODAY, April 21, 2010, http://www.usatoday.com/news/politics/2010
-04-20-independents_N.htm.
12. Jeffrey Jones, "Republican, Democratic Party Favorability Identical at 44%,"
Gallup Politics, September 23, 2010, http://www.gallup.com/poll/143213/
republican-democratic-party-favorability-identical.aspx.
13. Wolf, "Frustrated Voters Cut Ties with Democrats, Republicans."
14. Jean-Francois Revel, *How Democracies Perish* (Garden City, NY: Doubleday,
1984).
15. Akhil Amar, presenting at Civic Collaboratory Conference. Seattle, WA, July
2011.

TWO
The Disappearing Dream

1. Votes Database. "110th Congress/Senate Members Voting with Their Parties,"*Washington Post,* n.d., http://www.ulysseek.comcached?idx=0&id=789516.
2. George Will, "A Politician for the High Court?," *Washington Post,* April 15,
2010.
3. Peter Baker, "Hip, Hip—If Not Hooray—for a Standstill Nation," *New York
Times,* June 18, 2011.
4. Walter McDougall, *The Constitutional History of U.S. Foreign Policy: 222 Years of
Tension in the Twilight Zone* (Philadelphia: Foreign Policy Research Institute,
2010), http://www.fpri.org/pubs/2010/McDougall.ConstitutionalHistoryUS
ForeignPolicy.pdf.

THREE
Reclaiming Our Democracy

1. John Avlon, "Christine O'Donnell: Exhibit A for Getting Rid of Closed Primaries," CNN, September 18, 2011, http://www.cnn.com/2011/09/18/opinion/avlon-partisan-primaries/index.html.
2. Geoffrey Stone, "Induction Symposium: American Institutions and a Civil Society," *American Academy of Arts & Sciences Bulletin*, Winter 2012.
3. Center for Range Voting, http://rangevoting.org/BallAccess.html (accessed March 11, 2012).
4. Norman Ornstein, "Ending the Permanent Campaign," *Boston Review*, May/June 2011.

FOUR
Drawing a Line in the Sand

1. Jim Cooper, "Fixing Congress," *Boston Review*, May/June 2011.
2. Aaron C. Davis, "Maryland Senate Approves Gov. Martin O'Malley's Redistricting Map, 33 to 13," *Washington Post*, October 18, 2011, http://www.washingtonpost.com/local/md-politics/maryland-senate-approves-gov-martin-omalleys-redistricting-map-33-to-13/2011/10/18/gIQALImjvL_story.html.
3. Will Weissert, "Texas Redistricting: Court Won't Block Map Challenged by GOP Attorney General Greg Abbott," Huffington Post, November 25, 2011, http://www.huffingtonpost.com/2011/11/26/texas-redistricting-map-court-republicans-minorities_n_1113996.html.
4. Danny Hayes and Seth C. McKee, "The Intersection of Redistricting, Race, and Participation," *American Journal of Political Science* 56, no. 15 (January 2012), 115–30, http://onlinelibrary.wiley.com/doi/10.1111/j.1540-5907.2011.00546.x/full.
5. William Galston, "Economic Growth and Institutional Innovation: Outlines of a Reform Agenda," Brookings Institution, Policy Brief Series 172, June 2010, http://www.brookings.edu/papers/2010/0601_innovation_galston.aspx.
6. Gregory Korte, "Eyes on Ariz. as Redistricting Panel Shaken Up," *USA Today*, November 3, 2011, www.usatoday.com/news/politics/story/2011-11-03/arizona-redistricting-commission-firing/51066052/1.

FIVE
The Money Stream

1. Jim Cooper, "Fixing Congress," *Boston Review*, May/June 2011.
2. Erika Lovley, "Can Nancy Pelosi Retake the House?," Politico, Nov. 15, 2011,

http://www.politico.com/arena/archive/can-nancy-pelosi-retake-the-house
.html.

3. Nick Nyhart, "The Demand for Campaign Cash," *Boston Review*, May/June 2011.

4. Matthew Murray, "NRCC Chides PACs: Walden Keeps Eye on Giving," *Roll Call*, April 20, 2010.

5. Nicholas Confessore, "Outside Groups Eclipsing G.O.P. as Hub of Campaigns," *New York Times*, October 29, 2011.

6. Anna Palmer and Jim VandeHei, "A New Way to Buy Real Influence," Politico, October 24, 2011, http://www.politico.com/news/stories/1011/66673.html.

7. Dan Eggen, "Influence Industry: New Ad Shows Cozy Ties Between Super PACs and Candidates," *Washington Post*, November 16, 2011.

8. Confessore, "Outside Groups Eclipsing G.O.P. as Hub of Campaigns."

9. Ruth Marcus, "Obama's Dive into the Super PAC Deep End," *Washington Post*, February 14, 2012.

10. Palmer and VandeHei, "A New Way to Buy Real Influence."

11. "Presidential Public Financing System FAQ," Common Cause, http://www.commoncause.org/site/pp.asp?c=dkLNK1MQIwG&b=1389223 (accessed March 10, 2012).

12. Michael Malbin, Norman J. Ornstein, and Thomas E. Mann, *Vital Statistics on Congress 2008* (Washington, DC: Brookings Institution Press, 2008).

13. *The Public and Broadcasting: How to Get the Most Service from Your Local Station*, Federal Communications Commission, Washington, DC, July 2008, http://transition.fcc.gov/mb/audio/decdoc/public_and_broadcasting.html.

SIX

Government Leaders, Not Party Leaders

1. William McKay and Charles W. Johnson, *Parliament and Congress: Representation and Scrutiny in the Twenty-First Century* (New York: Oxford University Press, 2010).

2. Don Wolfensberger, "Leadership Control Is Faulted for House Ills," *Roll Call*, December 13, 2010.

3. Byron York, "Dems Turn Risky Health Vote into Manhood Contest," *Washington Examiner*, March 5, 2010.

4. *Setting Course: A Congressional Management Guide* (Washington, DC: Congressional Management Foundation, n.d.).

5. Ronald Brownstein, "Pulling Apart," *National Journal*, February 27, 2011.

6. Kathryn Pearson, "The Deep Roots of Polarization," *Boston Review*, May/June 2011.

7. Walter Oleszek and Richard Sachs, "Speakers Reed, Cannon, and Gingrich: Catalysts of Institutional and Procedural Change," in *The Cannon Centenary Conference: The Changing Nature of the Speakership*, ed. Walter J. Oleszek (Washington, DC: Government Printing Office, 2004), 128–40, http://www .gpoaccess.gov/serialset/cdocuments/hd108-204/pdf/fulldoc.pdf.
8. Jim Cooper, "Fixing Congress," *Boston Review*, May/June 2011.
9. "Carlos J. Moorhead," *Washington Post*, November 30, 2011.
10. Barbara Sinclair, *Party Wars: Polarization and the Politics of National Policy Making* (Norman: University of Oklahoma Press, 2006).
11. Sean Theriault, *Party Polarization in Congress* (New York: Cambridge University Press, 2008).
12. Ibid.
13. Jackie Kucinich, "Female GOP Committee Leaders Are a Rarity in the House," *The Hill*, October 5, 2005.
14. Kathryn Pearson, "The Deep Roots of Polarization," *Boston Review*, May/June 2011.

SEVEN

Debate and Democracy

1. Stanley Bach and Steven Smith, *Managing Uncertainty in the House of Representatives* (Washington, DC: Brookings Institution, 1988).
2. Rules Committee Majority Staff, "Open Rules by the Numbers," House Rules Committee, June 1, 2011, http://rules.house.gov/News/BlogArticle.aspx?News ID=327.
3. Don Wolfensberger, "Leadership Control Is Faulted for House Ills," *Roll Call*, December 13, 2010.
4. Ibid.
5. Sean Theriault, *Party Polarization in Congress* (New York: Cambridge University Press, 2008).
6. John Avlon, "How Obama Can Win," The Daily Beast, November 5, 2011, http://www.thedailybeast.com/articles/2011/11/04/john-avlon-how-obama -can-reelection-through-reform-of-congress.html.

NINE

Rivals, Not Enemies

1. *Setting Course: A Congressional Management Guide*, edition for the 112th Congress (Washington, DC: Congressional Management Foundation, 2010).

TEN

The Partisan Presidency

1. Ezra Klein, "Why Obama Is No FDR," *Washington Post*, November 8, 2011.

ELEVEN

Declarations of Independence

1. John Avlon, *Independent Nation: How Centrism Can Change American Politics* (New York: Three Rivers Press, 2005).
2. John Kennedy, *Profiles in Courage* (New York: Perennial, 2000).
3. Russell Berman and Bernie Becker, "Norquist's Group Won't Remove Names of House Members Disavowing Tax Pledge," *The Hill*, November 9, 2011.
4. Brooks, "The Two Moons," *New York Times*, November 21, 2011.

TWELVE

Beyond Partisanship

1. Daniel Klein, "I Was Wrong, and So Are You," *Atlantic*, December 2011.
2. David Souter, "Induction Symposium: American Institutions and a Civil Society," *American Academy of Arts and Sciences Bulletin*, Winter 2012.
3. Eric Hoffer, *The True Believer: Thoughts on the Nature of Mass Movements* (New York: Perennial, 1989).
4. Eric Hoffer, "Thoughts of Eric Hoffer, Including: 'Absolute Faith Corrupts Absolutely,'" *New York Times Magazine*, April 25, 1971.
5. Amy Gutmann and Dennis Thompson, "How to Free Congress's Mind," *New York Times*, November 29, 2011.
6. Rosalind Helderman, "Congress Struggles to Fix Budget Gridlock as Another Deadline Looms," *Washington Post*, October 26, 2011.

THIRTEEN

The Way Forward

1. Norman Ornstein, "Ending the Permanent Campaign," *Boston Review*, May/June 2011.
2. Elizabeth Garrett, "Direct Democracy and Public Choice." Research Paper No. C08-16, USC Center in Law, Economics and Organization, Los Angeles, 2009.
3. Mickey Edwards, "How to Turn Republicans and Democrats into Americans," *Atlantic*, July/August 2011.

Suggested Reading

The ideas in this book are my own, but as is always the case they are the product of input from many sources. If one wishes to tackle big issues, the best place to start is by a thorough immersion in the works of others who have thought about the same things, sometimes planting seeds that yield important insights and sometimes forcing you to rethink critical assumptions. "Democracy" is a big canvas on which to paint, but every painting is made up of many smaller brushstrokes. In the reading list I propose here you will find reflections on democracy, on elections, on governance, on politics, on society, on relationships, all of which make up a piece of the puzzle as to how to create a sustainable system of self-government. Even a quick glance at some of these titles and the names of the authors will alert you that some of these volumes do not reflect my own conclusions on the issues they explore. But as I suggest in this book, if you listen only to those who already agree with you, you are not likely to gain much. I'm indebted to the men and women who labored over these books and thus helped me increase my own understanding of the nature of the problems we face, the root causes of those problems, and some possible paths out of the thicket in which we find ourselves.

Avlon, John P. *Independent Nation.* New York: Harmony Books, 2004.

Barry, John M. *The Ambition and the Power: The Fall of Jim Wright.* New York: Penguin-Viking, 1989.

Bishop, Bill. *The Big Sort.* New York: Houghton-Mifflin, 2008.

Bok, Derek. *The State of the Nation: Government and the Quest for a Better Society.* Cambridge, MA: Harvard University Press, 1996.

Breyer, Stephen. *Making Our Democracy Work.* New York: Knopf, 2010.

Brownstein, Ronald. *The Second Civil War: How Extreme Partisanship Has Paralyzed Washington and Polarized America.* New York: Penguin, 2007.

Connelly, William Jr. *James Madison Rules America: The Constitutional Origins of Congressional Partisanship.* Lanham, MD: Rowman & Littlefield, 2010.

Devins, Neal, and Louis Fisher. *The Democratic Constitution.* New York: Oxford University Press, 2004.

Eggers, William D., and John O'Leary. *If We Can Put a Man on the Moon: Getting Big Things Done in Government.* Cambridge, MA: Harvard University Press, 2009.

Eilperin, Juliet. *Fight Club Politics: How Partisanship Is Poisoning the House of Representatives.* Lanham, MD: Rowman & Littlefield, 2006.

Heclo, Hugh. *On Thinking Institutionally.* Boulder, CO: Paradigm, 2008.

Hudson, William E. *American Democracy in Peril: Seven Challenges to America's Future.* Chatham, NJ: Chatham House, 1995.

Hughes, Robert. *Culture of Complaint: The Fraying of America.* New York: Oxford University Press, 1993.

Lapham, Lewis H. *The Wish for Kings: Democracy at Bay.* New York: Grove Press, 1993.

Lee, Frances. *Beyond Ideology: Politics, Principles, and Partisanship in the United States Senate.* Chicago: University of Chicago Press, 2009.

Lukacs, John. *Democracy and Populism: Fear and Hatred.* New Haven: Yale University Press, 2005.

Mann, Thomas E., and Norman J. Ornstein. *The Broken Branch: How Congress Is Failing America and How to Get It Back on Track.* New York: Oxford University Press, 2006.

Mansbridge, Jane J. *Beyond Adversary Democracy.* Chicago: University of Chicago Press, 1983.

Mutz, Diana C. *Hearing the Other Side: Deliberative Versus Participatory Democracy.* Cambridge, MA: Cambridge University Press, 2006.

Obey, David. *Raising Hell for Justice: The Washington Battles of a Heartland Progressive.* Madison: University of Wisconsin Press, 2007.

Polsby, Nelson. *How Congress Evolves: Social Bases of Institutional Change.* Oxford: Oxford University Press, 2004.

Putnam, Robert D. *Bowling Alone: The Collapse and Revival of American Community.* New York: Simon and Schuster, 2000.

Rakove, Jack N. *Original Meanings: Politics and Ideas in the Making of the Constitution.* New York: Knopf, 1996.

Rodin, Judith, and Stephen P. Steinberg (eds.). *Public Discourse in America: Conversation and Community in the Twenty-first Century.* Philadelphia: University of Pennsylvania Press, 2003.

Sabl, Andrew. *Ruling Passions: Political Offices and Democratic Ethics.* Princeton, NJ: Princeton University Press, 2002.

Theriault, Sean M. *Party Polarization in Congress.* New York: Cambridge University Press, 2008.

Thompson, Dennis F. *Just Elections: Creating a Fair Electoral Process in the United States.* Chicago: Chicago University Press, 2002.

Wolfe, Alan. *Does American Democracy Still Work?* New Haven: Yale University Press, 2006.

Wright, Jim. *Balance of Power: Presidents and Congress from the Era of McCarthy to the Age of Gingrich.* Atlanta: Turner Publishing, 1996.

Yankelovich, Daniel. *The Magic of Dialogue: Transforming Conflict into Cooperation.* New York: Simon and Schuster, 1999.

Index

Index

Stewart, Jimmy, 117, 118
stimulus spending, xiii–xiv, 26,
    162–63
Stockman, David, 98
Stone, Geoffrey, xii–xiii, 41–42
strategic voting, 46
"supercommittee," 167
super-PACs, 71, 74, 75, 76–77
Supreme Court: campaign finance
    decisions by, 71, 82; nomina-
    tions to, xiv, 165; primary elec-
    tion decisions by, 52–53; redis-
    tricting decisions by, 59

talk radio, 30, 95
tariffs, 47
taxes, xiv, 7, 9, 43, 80, 95, 150,
    153–54, 155, 166–67
Tea Party, 9, 174, 175, 176
telephone banks, 73
television, 73, 83–85
Tennessee, 67
term limits: for congressional
    committee chairs, 101; for
    elected officials, 92
Texas, 52–53; gerrymandering in,
    57, 59, 62
Theriault, Sean, 106, 116, 127
third parties, 14, 46–47, 52
Thomas, Clarence, 23
Thomas, Craig, 21
Thompson, Dennis, 165
Thurmond, Strom, 118, 120
Toomey, Mike, 75
Toomey, Pat, 41

town hall meetings, 11, 177–78
trade agreements, 28, 138
travel restrictions, 137–38
treaties, 138
True Believer, The (Hoffer), 164
Truman, Harry, 93
turnout, of voters, xviii, 6, 14, 42,
    54, 63, 66
Twitter, 83, 179

unemployment, 175
unions, 71, 86
Utah, 39

VandeHei, Jim, 75
Virginia, 73
Vital Statistics on Congress, 82
voice votes, 172
Voinovich, George, 21
voters: Independent, 10–11; resil-
    iency of, x; turnout of, xviii, 6,
    14, 42, 54, 63, 66
voting, 16–17; by House mem-
    bers, 172; "instant runoff," 47;
    mandatory, 53–54; schedule
    for, 54–55; strategic, 46; write-
    in, 45

Waiting for Superman (documen-
    tary), 40
Walden, Greg, 72
Walker, Bob, 77
Walsh, Brian, 75
war, xix, 7, 20, 43, 80, 112, 138,
    150, 153